EVOLUTION
AS A
RELIGION

Strange hopes
and stranger fears

EVOLUTION

AS A

RELIGION,

Strange hopes
and stranger fears

MARY MIDGLEY

METHUEN   London and New York

First published in 1985 by
Methuen & Co. Ltd
11 New Fetter Lane
London EC4P 4EE

Published in the USA by
Methuen & Co.
in association with Methuen, Inc.
29 West 35th Street
New York, NY 10001

© 1985 Mary Midgley

Photoset by
Rowland Phototypesetting Ltd,
Bury St Edmunds, Suffolk
Printed in Great Britain
at the University Press, Cambridge

*British Library Cataloguing in
Publication Data*

Midgley, Mary
    Evolution as a religion : strange
    hopes and stranger fears.
    1. Evolution—Philosophy
    I. Title
    116   QH366.2

    ISBN 0-416-39650-x
    ISBN 0-416-39660-7 Pbk

*Library of Congress Cataloging in
Publication Data*

Midgley, Mary, 1919–
    Evolution as a religion.

    Bibliography: p.
    Includes index.
    1. Evolution—Religious
    aspects.   2. Religion and
    science—1946–   . II. Title.
    BL263.M485
    1985   213   815-13893
    ISBN 0-416-39650-x
    ISBN 0-416-39660-7 (pbk.)

To the Memory of Charles Darwin
Who Did Not Say These Things

Erratum
Page 59, line 16: For 'Jewish' read 'Jesuit'.

Contents ——————————

Acknowledgements —————————

This book has grown out of an article of the same name published by Basil Blackwell in 1985 in a book called *Darwinism and Divinity*, edited by John Durant. I am grateful to the publishers for permission to reprint its scattered elements here. The only other parts which have appeared before are as follows: in chapter 17, about half of an article called 'Towards a new understanding of human nature; the limits of individualism', published in *How Humans Adapt; A Biocultural Odyssey* (edited by Donald J. Ortner) by the Smithsonian Institution Press, Washington, D.C. 20560, USA in 1983, has been reworked. Chapter 18 appeared, almost as now, in *Encounter* (February 1983) under the title 'Duties concerning islands'. Chapters 14 and 15 contain scattered parts of an article called 'De-dramatizing Darwinism', published in *The Monist*, 67, 2 (April 1984). I am grateful to all those concerned with these publications for their kind permission to reprint.

I have had a great deal of help from my family, friends and colleagues in this project which has proved unusually interdisciplinary and confusing. I would specially like to acknowledge the help of Ann Loades, Alec Panchen, Sylvia Feinmann, John Durant and David Midgley.

1
Evolutionary dramas

There is grandeur in this view of life.

Charles Darwin

Science and symbolism

The theory of evolution is not just an inert piece of theoretical science. It is, and cannot help being, also a powerful folk-tale about human origins. Any such narrative must have symbolic force. We are probably the first culture not to make that its main function. Most stories about human origins must have been devised purely with a view to symbolic and poetic fittingness. Suggestions about how we were made and where we come from are bound to engage our imagination, to shape our views of what we now are, and so to affect our lives. Scientists, when they find themselves caught up in these webs of symbolism, sometimes complain, calling for a sanitary cordon to keep them away from science. But this seems to be both psychologically and logically impossible.

Our theoretical curiosity simply is not detached in this way from the rest of our life. Nor do scientists themselves always want it to be so. Some of the symbolic webs are ones which they approve of, and promote as part of the ideal of science itself. For instance, Jacques Monod, as an atheistical biochemist, does not just rejoice at getting rid of the theistic drama. He at once replaces it by another drama, just as vivid, emotive and relevant to life, in which Sartrian man appears as the lonely hero challenging an alien and meaningless universe:

> It is perfectly true that science attacks values. Not directly, since science is no judge of them and *must* ignore them; but it subverts

every one of the mythical or philosophical ontogenies upon which the animist tradition, from the Australian aborigines to the dialectical materialists, has based morality, values, duties, rights, prohibitions.

If he accepts this message in its full significance, man must at last wake out of his millenary dream and discover his total solitude, his fundamental isolation. He must realize that, like a gypsy, he lives on the boundary of an alien world; a world that is deaf to his music, and as indifferent to his hopes as it is to his sufferings or his crimes.[1]

But 'discovering his total solitude' is just adopting one imaginative stance among many possible ones. Other good scientists, very differently, have used the continuity of our species with the rest of the physical world to reprove human arrogance and to call for practical recognition of kinship with other creatures. Many, like Darwin and the great geneticist Theodosius Dobzhansky, have held that an attitude of awe and veneration for the wonders of the physical world is an essential condition for studying them properly. Others have talked in a more predatory way about the joys of the chase and the triumph of catching facts. Both motives, and many others, are evidently so habitual in science that they are only not mentioned because they are taken for granted.

It seems often to be assumed that they are therefore irrelevant, that Science itself is something so pure and impersonal that it ought to be thought of in complete abstraction from all the motives that might lead people to practise it. This, unfortunately, cannot work because of the importance of world-pictures. Facts are not gathered in a vacuum, but to fill gaps in a world-picture which already exists. And the shape of this world-picture – determining the matters allowed for it, the principles of selection, the possible range of emphases – depends deeply on the motives for forming it in the first place.

Imagination, which guides thought, is directed by our attitudes. For instance, predatory and competitive motives tend to produce a picture dominated by competition and predation – one in which these elements do not only play their part, as they did for Darwin, but are arbitrarily and dogmatically isolated as sole rulers. Thus, in a familiar distortion which will concern us repeatedly, the sociobiologist M. T. Ghiselin flatly declares:

The evolution of society fits the Darwinian paradigm in its most individualistic form. The economy of nature is competitive from beginning to end. Understand that economy, and how it works, and the underlying reasons for social phenomena are manifest. They are the means by which one organism gains some advantage to the detriment of another. No hint of genuine charity ameliorates our vision of society, once sentimentalism has been laid aside. What passes for co-operation turns out to be a mixture of opportunism and exploitation. The impulses that lead one animal to sacrifice himself for another turn out to have their ultimate rationale in gaining advantage over a third, and acts for the good of one 'society' turn out to be performed for the detriment of the rest. Where it is in his own interest, every organism my reasonably be expected to aid his fellows. Where he has no alternative, he submits to the yoke of servitude. Yet, given a full chance to act in his own interest, nothing but expediency will restrain him from brutalizing, from maiming, from murdering – his brother, his mate, his parent, or his child. Scratch an 'altruist' and watch a 'hypocrite' bleed.[2]

As we shall see, this claim is essentially pure fantasy, not only unsupported by the empirical facts which are supposed to be its grounds, but actually contrary to them, such as they are. Is this a quite exceptional aberration? Some will suspect that it must be, not only because the world-picture involved is a bad one, but because scientists ought to be so impartial that they either do not have anything so unprofessional as a world-picture at all, or, if they have one, do not let it affect their work.

But this is a mistaken ideal. An enquirer with no such general map would only be an obsessive – someone who had a special motive for collecting facts indiscriminately. He would not be a person without an attitude, or without special motives, but one with motives so odd as to inhibit the kind of organizing activity which normally shapes people's ideas into some sort of coherent whole. Merely to pile up information indiscriminately is an idiot's task. Good scientists do not approximate to that ideal at all. They tend to have a very strong guiding imaginative system. Their world-picture is usually a positive and distinctive one, with its own special drama. They do not scrupulously avoid conveying any sense of dark and light, of what matters and what does not, of what is to be aimed at and what avoided at all costs. They use the lights and shadows to reveal the landscape. Like those who argue usefully on any other subject, they do their best work not by being neutral but by having strong preferences, being aware of them, criticizing them carefully, expressing them plainly and then leaving their readers to decide how far to share them.

Symbolism, then, is not just a nuisance to be got rid of. It is essential. Facts will never appear to us as brute and meaningless; they will always organize themselves into some sort of story, some drama. These dramas can indeed be dangerous. They can distort our theories, and they have distorted the theory of evolution perhaps more than any other. The only way in which we can control this kind of distortion is, I believe, to bring the dramas themselves out into the open, to give them our full attention, understand them better and see what part, if any, each of them ought to play both in theory and in life. It is no use merely to swipe at them from time to time, like troublesome insects, while officially attending only to the theoretical questions. This will not make them go away, because they are a serious feature of life.

Darwin's balance

The drama that attends a theory need not, then, be mere melodrama. When sensationalism is present it is either irrelevant or – if it really belongs to a theory – shows that that theory is bad. The drama that goes with a good theory is simply the expressive aspect of the theory itself. In order of time, it is often conceived in advance of much of the supporting evidence. But when further facts accumulate, it ought to respond to them by refining and subtilizing its cruder outlines. This process usually makes it less extreme and one-sided, and so moves it away from the gratuitous sensationalism which marks melodrama. That does not make it less stirring or less important for life; it can make it more so. This imaginative and emotional deepening is part of the growth of a theory, not just a chance ornament. When the young Darwin immersed himself in the arguments about cosmic purpose in Paley's theological textbook *The Evidences of Christianity*, and repeatedly read *Paradise Lost* on exploring trips from the *Beagle*,[3] he was neither wasting his time nor distorting his scientific project. He was seriously working his way through a range of life-positions which lay on the route to the one he could finally use.

The result of this long preliminary pilgrimage was to make his own picture unusually balanced and inclusive. To keep it so is, however, terribly hard. He himself made clear that he felt this difficulty deeply, and was constantly dissatisfied with his efforts, constantly changing his books to do justice to some neglected angle. The vastness of the truth and the one-sidedness of formulae always haunted him. This haunting by no means reduced his work to an undramatic neutrality. Instead, the tension of opposites makes the drama which he shows us comprehensive and Shakespearian, so that it includes every mood. Gillian Beer has lately pointed out how rich his style is in fertile metaphors and models, which he continually uses to supplement and correct each other.[4] Centrally, he will not lose hold of either of the two emotional responses which belong most naturally to evolutionary speculation – on the one hand, optimistic, joyful wonder at the profusion of nature, and on the other, pessimistic, sombre alarm at its wasteful cruelty. Since he cannot qualify every sentence, selective quotation often makes him seem enslaved to one or other of these attitudes. And others who have made real efforts to come to terms with the conflict have been misrepresented in the same sort of way.

No malice is needed for this distortion. Even given goodwill, the difficulty is immense. What is needed is not just a set of rules for handling factual disputes, of the kind which is recognized as part of scientific training. Since this vast issue involves our whole view of our place in the world, discussion of it calls out and reflects the whole shape of the character. The way in which we treat it inevitably reveals our weaknesses and prejudices. Dozens of awkward truths about ourselves are relevant to this subject; our avoidance of any of them projects a distortion on to the screen of our theory. Obviously we shall never escape their influence. What is needed is the kind of effort which Darwin made to become aware of them, to separate them from the more narrowly factual issues, and to watch out for their dangers.

Am I exaggerating these dangers? Some physical scientists are likely to feel that the kind of thing I have been describing does indeed happen in other disciplines, notably in the humanities, but does not normally happen in their own, and cannot really have mattered to Darwin. I only wish that they were right. The destructive message of this book is a somewhat dismal one. It concerns the sort of trouble which arises when, with writers less careful than Darwin, the dramas take over. About evolution, theory itself has again and again been distorted by biases flowing from over-simple, unbalanced world-pictures. The trouble does not, of course, lie in mere wish-fulfilment of the obvious kind which paints the world as we should like it to be. It involves being obsessed by a picture so colourful and striking that it numbs thought about the evidence required to support it. Standards of proof then fall headlong. Half the trouble of course takes place out of sight, in the mere choice of problems, in taking some things for granted and being quite unpersuadable about others, in unconsciously placing the burden of proof on one's opponents, and sometimes in pure tribal feeling which confines one's attention to the fellow-specialists who already share one's premisses. Of course it is true that the resulting mistakes are usually not as bad as the exaggerated forms in which they are reflected by outsiders, and also that they are 'not part of science'. Mistakes never are. But since what is needed in order to correct them is not to avoid all world-pictures altogether, but to form better ones, this whole process is a matter for real scientific concern.

False lights

There are two distortions in particular which will mainly concern us in this book, and they had better be indicated, however crudely, right away. Neither is new; both have often been denounced. But both persist, not just in the minds of outsiders ignorant of evolutionary theory, but also in those of many scientists who develop and expound it. The first is the better known and the more obviously pernicious. It is the 'Social Darwinist' idea, expressed by Ghiselin, that life has been scientifically proved to be essentially competitive, in some sense which exposes all social feeling as somehow mere humbug and illusion. The phrase 'survival of the fittest' has been used, ever since Herbert Spencer first coined it, to describe an individualistic law showing such things as co-operation, love and altruism to be unreal, a law which (somewhat mysteriously) both demands and predicts that they should always give way to self-interest. This has often been exposed as nonsense. Since many very successful species of social animals, including our own, have evolved these traits, have survived by them and continue to live by them, their unreality cannot be the message of evolutionary theory. But because of its strong dramatic force, as well as various political uses, this notion persists through repeated attempts to correct it, and often twists up the ideas even of those who think they are helping to get rid of it. It is especially troublesome in the American sociobiology debate, a topic to which I shall have to give a rather disproportionate amount of attention, simply because its wide publicity makes it, just now, the most prominent hotbed of noisy errors about evolution.

The second main distortion may be called Panglossism, or the Escalator Fallacy. It is the idea that evolution is a steady, linear upward movement, a single inexorable process of improvement, leading (as a disciple of Herbert Spencer's put it) 'from gas to genius'[5] and beyond into some superhuman spiritual stratosphere. This idea, first put forward by Jean-Baptiste Lamarck at the beginning of the century,[6] convinced Spencer instantly and completely. It did not convince Darwin at all. He thought it vacuous, pointed out the obscurity of the metaphor 'higher', and relied on no such paid-up cosmic insurance policy to bail out the human race. He developed his own view of selection on the humbler model of a bush – a rich radiation of varying forms, in which human qualities cannot, any more than any others, determine a general direction for the whole. Here too, however, what he rejected has been kept by many people as a central feature of the idea of evolution and seen as a key part of 'Darwinism'. Still unsupported by argument, it too continues to produce some extremely strange theorizing, and in its less obvious way also to do a great deal of damage. These two kinds of drama are, in fact, the shapes into which the two main strands of feeling about evolution naturally develop, if they are not held in balance and forced to correct each other. They are the hypertrophied forms of cosmic optimism and cosmic pessimism respectively. Since both these moods are common, theory-builders often oscillate between them rather casually, and produce views which owe something to both. Unluckily, this is not the same thing as the synthesis which Darwin attempted. It can merely give us the worst of both worlds.

The fear of biology

Melodramas like these, especially the 'Social Darwinist' or Spencerist one, account, I am sure, for the strong objection which many people still feel to seriously taking the theory of evolution on board at all. This objection is not confined to Biblical creationists. Certainly the persistence of creationism, leading to a recent expansion and even the conversion of a few physical scientists, itself indicates something beyond mere passive conservatism. But what is much more interesting and important is the subtler resistance still common among social scientists. This is not a denial of evolutionary theory itself, which is usually conceded as correct in its own sphere, but a steady rejection of any attempt to use it in the interpretation of human affairs. A sanitary cordon is erected at the frontier between the physical and social sciences, at which biological explanations generally and evolutionary ones in particular still tend to be turned back, marked with an official stamp which may read 'Fascist', 'Racist', 'Galtonist', 'Innatist', 'Biological Determinist', or at times, most grimly of all, merely 'Biological'.

This habit is fortunately on the way out, and a modest two-way traffic does now go on, to the general advantage. But a good deal of work is still needed to explain – as is always necessary in these cases – the distortions which gave rise to the prejudice in the first place, and just why they are not actually part of biological science. That is a main business of this book.

Tribally speaking, this debate is conceived as a border dispute between social scientists and biologists. It can appear to be one between their respective sciences themselves. Since, however, sciences cannot oppose each other in this way, there is plainly a need for rethinking and restatement when their representatives start doing so. It is helpful, I think, to begin by looking at the historical reasons why inter-science war at this point did not surprise or shock people as much as it ought to have done.

In the first place, within the social sciences themselves, disputes about the sources of human conduct have often been somewhat aggressively and competitively conducted. There is a real difficulty in grasping the vastness of the subject, in seeing that distinct insights need not be rivals, but can explain different aspects of life, and can eventually be compatible. In this way physical explanations have chronically been seen as competing with psychological ones, introspection as competing with laboratory work, observation with experiment, interest in heredity with interest in environment, history with science, and answers to large questions with answers to small ones. In this competitive atmosphere, the standing of biological explanations was also much injured by their repeated misuse during the last century for sinister political purposes. Starting from Francis Galton's eugenic proposals to weed out the lower classes, as well as non-European races, by selective breeding, oppressors repeatedly invoked the name and prestige of biology, along with Social Darwinist distortions of evolutionary theory, to justify exploitation. The notion of fitness was twisted to preserve white dominance in the United States through so-called intelligence testing, bolstered by false, but seductive, biological theories.[7] It also figured in the ravings of the Nazis. Thus biology itself became associated in the public mind with a string of indefensible right-wing positions. Since these people's biological theories were usually false, based on views of (for instance) race which were not biological at all, this hijacking ought no more to have discredited genuine biology than the errors of alchemists discredit chemistry. The association is a quite external one. It is in fact just as easy to misuse environmentalist theories for oppressive purposes. For instance, J. B. Watson, the founder of behaviourist psychology, did this in recommending his perverse and inhuman system of baby-care.[8] And the whole notion of natural human tastes which rulers must not distort or ignore – a notion on which we all rest when we resist bad institutions as 'inhuman' – presupposes a firm biological basis in inherited human nature. Marx's central notion of 'dehumanization' rests on this plinth, and his attacks on the notion of human nature are simply aimed at inadequate forms of it. If there were no such thing as human nature, the objections to a *Brave New World* existence could never arise. Conditioning is the tool of tyrants. Natural, inborn human spontaneity, seeking a more satisfying life even among people who have been brutally conditioned to know nothing but slavery, is the source of resistance to tyranny. It is the myths, not real biological theory, which have associated our evolutionary origins with injustice and oppression. That is why it is so important to expose them.

This irrelevance of bad political doctrines to real biological theory has been the theme of a great deal that I have written, and I must not repeat those discussions here.[9] One feature of the present enquiry, however, is different. Previously I have been largely occupied with myths which seemed to be deforming the social sciences; here I deal mainly with ones infesting the physical ones. I hope it will be clear, in the one case as in the other, that this is no more an attack on those sciences themselves than an exposure of forged money is an attack on the Mint or a denunciation of quack remedies is an attack on the medical profession. I have been heartened by the readiness of a number of scientific colleagues to make this distinction, and I very much hope that readers will be willing to put themselves to the same trouble, for which I thank them.

2

Do science and religion compete?

If a general council of the Church Scientific had been held at that time, we should have been condemned by an overwhelming majority.

T. H. Huxley

The Wilberforce legend

Political feuds, however, are hardy plants, very difficult to weed out of a controversy once they have got into it. And this particular controversy was already distorted by animosities drawn from an older warfare, that which has been conceived as raging between science and religion in the nineteenth century, centrally over the theory of evolution. That seems to have been the point at which the idea of evolution, and to some extent of science generally, began to be seen as immoral and inhuman, while scientists began, in reply, to see notions of morality and humanity as anti-scientific and obscurantist. The whole idea of this warfare is a very strange one, and it is part of our business in this book to understand it better.

It is very interesting to notice how far later tradition has exaggerated the Victorian dispute and distorted our view of its nature. As James Moore has shown,[1] it certainly did not appear at the time as raging between science and religion, but as cutting straight across both. Darwin's most serious opponents by far were the official scientific establishment of his day and many of his supporters, such as Charles Kingsley and H. G. Baden-Powell, were clergymen — as were, after all, many of those scientists who had already established the far from Biblical age of the earth. More remarkably still, however, it turns out that the one thing we all thought we did know about, the famous confrontation between Thomas Henry Huxley, acting as 'Darwin's bull-dog', and Bishop Wilberforce in 1860, is something that we do not know about at all. Contemporary accounts do not bear out the version of it we were brought up on. Wilberforce (it emerges) certainly did not just waffle and appeal to irrelevant feeling. He made clear, forceful and pertinent scientific criticisms, which were seen as such by Darwin himself. (Darwin at once began experimental work to answer them.) Wilberforce was, after all, not present as a bishop but as a scientist, vice-president of the British Academy, with good ornithological work to his credit, and spokesman for Sir Richard Owen, the greatest anatomist of the day. In his review of the *Origin* just before, he had written:

> We are too loyal pupils of inductive philosophy to start back from any conclusion by reason of its strangeness. . . . We have no sympathy with those who object to any facts or alleged facts in Nature, or to any inference logically deduced from them, because they believe them to contradict what it appears to them is taught by Revelation.[2]

He could scarcely have dropped these principles at Oxford without attracting comment. Just what he did finally say to upset Huxley we shall probably never now know. Neither his remark nor Huxley's reply was sufficiently noticed to be reported. The man who stood out at the time as having actually answered Wilberforce was the botanist Joseph Hooker. But his answers were, of course, limited by the fact that Darwin's theory at that time really did need a great deal more evidence and basic thought before it could be defended against critical scientists.

No dishonesty on the part of Huxley and his friends was needed to generate the later version. It grew naturally out of the hindsight of the victors. They simply forgot what Wilberforce had said. His scientific objections, which had been serious and necessary in their time, were dropped from memory once they had been answered. And all of us find it much easier to remember our own contribution to a debate than other people's. It is unfortunate, however, that two of Huxley's later preoccupations contributed to distort his memory of this actually rather trifling affair, and to make it look to him like a holy war. He spent much of his later life campaigning to establish professionalism in science, to move the occupational image away from that of a broad 'naturalist', which was how Darwin always described himself – a gentleman living on his private means or working as a clergyman – to that of a full-time, fully paid, specialized 'scientist'. And he also found himself, as an important Victorian sage, saying a great deal about the purpose and meaning of life which brought him into conflict with the

Church. Wilberforce therefore personified both Huxley's hates by being an amateur scientist as well as a bishop. This very fact, however, points to a paradox in Huxley's own position. In his own interests, he by no means confined himself to being merely an anatomist, or even merely an evolutionist. His thoughts ranged remarkably widely, and he certainly saw no need to draw a sharp line between even their widest ranges and his scientific views. He thought as a whole person, a person who was a scientist. And it seemed to him that it was essentially scientific business which brought him into conflict with religion. But on the narrower notions of science which have come out of his work, this can scarcely be right. Can there really be such a conflict?

Clashes due to trespass

In what sense can two such abstract entities as science and religion (or morality) be said to clash? Mere accidental personal feuds between their followers are not enough to justify this language. They can surely only clash where they compete, where they represent rival attempts to perform the same function. How far, if at all, can science and religion do this?

There is, of course, a well-known set of cases where they seem to do it, namely, where religion is invoked against science on a point of empirical fact. The literal acceptance of archaic Biblical ideas on cosmology is an obvious case. Creationists who attempt this are taking on a scientific task, as indeed they now recognize by their preference for talk of 'creation science'. But their reasons for undertaking it flow not from religion as such, nor even from Christianity, but from their own peculiar conception of the Bible as literally true and divinely dictated. Other Christians object to this view strongly, on the obvious grounds that it is needless, and moreover that the Bible, in spite of its grandeur, contains many things which conflict not just with science, but with morality, with history, with common sense or with each other. If there were a god who had dictated the whole of it, he would certainly not be one we ought to worship. Biblical writers seem, then, to have been as fallible and imperfect as other human beings, and moreover to have used – as would naturally be expected – a mythical and metaphorical way of writing where that was suitable, instead of making the quite irrelevant attempt to be modern physical scientists. The central objections to fundamentalist literalism are religious, moral and historical ones. If they are right, this is a case where 'religion' does not clash with science unless something has gone wrong with it already on its own terms. The religion which does clash with science has left its own sphere, for bad reasons, to intrude on a scientific one. It is bad religion.

This kind of case is relatively familiar and well understood. In this book, however, we shall be more concerned with the opposite kind, which has been less noticed. We shall look at doctrines which are believed to be scientific, but are not actually so, and whose persuasiveness seems to be due to their serving some of the functions of a religion, even though they are seen by their promoters as being hostile to 'religion' as such. Sometimes indeed they are put forward consciously as substitutes for religion, able to replace it in public acceptance. This project would hardly make sense if they were not seen as performing in some sense the same function, that is as being somehow religious doctrines in their own right, aimed essentially at the spiritual nourishment and salvation of the human race. The effect is doubly strange. These doctrines not only lack suitable arguments to recommend them in their new, salvationary role. They also conflict with the genuinely scientific theories which are supposed to provide their roots and to justify their name. Like 'creationist science' they offend against the laws of their country of origin even before attempting to conquer a wider territory. Bad religion is being answered by bad science. If we ask 'by what myths do people today support themselves?' we shall often find that they do it by myths which they wrongly suppose to be part of science.

The division of spheres

Does it follow, then, that religion and science never conflict so long as both are properly conducted? That would be a bold claim. We shall need to have a much clearer idea of both entities before we can approach it. But it does seem plain that many of their current supposed clashes are produced by confusion. That very clear-headed geneticist, Theodosius Dobzhansky, made a useful suggestion for dividing their spheres: 'Science and religion deal with different aspects of existence. If one dares to overschematize for the sake of clarity, one may say that these are the aspect of fact and the aspect of meaning.'[3] Since the notion that facts are the province of science is very widely accepted, this seems a reasonable suggestion. What, however, is the province of meaning?

Meaning and faith

Meaning is perhaps best thought of as the way in which facts connect to form what I have called world-pictures – that is the underlying systems of thought by which we order our experience. A meaningless 'brute' fact is one which we cannot fit into this system. And, if the system itself falls apart, that is when we say that our life has become meaningless. Experience is of course too complicated for these systems ever to become neat or complete. All the same, each of them has some kind of a central region. The more closely any particular fact is linked to this centre, and the more light it throws on the interconnections of the whole, the more meaning, significance or importance it has. This system, moreover, is as a whole related to purpose – our own purposes and others of which we are aware. Quite modestly, people often find plenty of meaning in their lives if they are working for their own purposes in harmony with those around them. In that situation, it is often artificial and misleading to ask whom a purpose belongs to. Each directly desires the satisfaction of the others and the fulfilment of joint projects. If we ask for a wider context – which many of us do – we begin to build wider intellectual systems, either just for greater completeness or to reconcile clashing elements within the system which we have already. All our more ambitious enquiries flow outwards from this central region.

Dobzhansky is surely right that this is the kind of work to which religion in general contributes. What, however, distinguishes religion from other sources of meaning? What makes a system a religious system, and how many religions are there?

This question can of course be dealt with in a very summary way by just referring to common practice. Thus, in the last war, when recruits were being asked for their religion on entering the forces, one of them was heard to reply, 'Marxist–Leninist–Dialectical–Materialist'. 'Can't spell it,' said the sergeant, 'put him down C. of E.' On this trouble-saving system, the title of this book is just a confusion. But this method leaves us with some serious questions unanswered. We know what the recruit meant. He was speaking of the faith he lived by. A faith is not primarily a factual belief, the acceptance of a few extra propositions like 'God exists' or 'there will be a revolution'. It is rather the sense of having one's place within a whole greater than oneself, one whose larger aims so enclose one's own and give them point that sacrifice for it may be entirely proper. This sense need not involve any extra factual beliefs at all. Marxism does not, nor does Taoism. Both call centrally for changes in attitude to the facts one already accepts – changes in connection, in emphasis, in attention, in selection, in the meaning and importance attached to particulars – in short, a changed world-picture. Sometimes changed opinions about facts will follow. Thus Marxism (but not Taoism) calls for a new set of expectations about the future. But even when there are such new opinions, it is not they but the attitude which generates them that is central. Converts

who only have the new factual beliefs and not the appropriate
attitudes will not last long.

This kind of faith is plainly something widespread and very
important in our lives. It need not be formalized at all. People, in fact,
often do not notice that they have it until whatever they have faith in –
perhaps their culture or their occupation – is threatened. But almost
everyone, however sceptical or uninterested in religion and metaphysics, has faith in something. Against religion, faith in science or in
reason is often invoked, and these go far beyond the existing successes.
People have faith in humanity, in democracy, in art, in medicine, in
economics or in western civilization, in trade – even, it seems, in
money, which is as odd an entity as any that religion has yet invented.
These faiths are not themselves religions, but they are the seedbed of
religions. In cultures where a strong, dominant religion already rules,
new minor faiths are simply absorbed into it as they arise. They are
not usually noticed unless they are so distinctive as to demand
widespread change. But in our own culture, where many people
officially have no religion at all, and those who have can chop and
change, new faiths have much more scope and can become more
distinctive. They are hungrily seized on by people whose lives lack
meaning. When this happens, there arise at once, unofficially and
spontaneously, many elements which we think of as characteristically
religious. We begin, for instance, to find priesthoods, prophecies,
devotion, bigotry, exaltation, heresy-hunting and sectarianism,
ritual, sacrifice, fanaticism, notions of sin, absolution and salvation,
and the confident promise of a heaven in the future.

Auguste Comte, the founder of positivism, whose 'religion of
humanity' displayed these and many other overtly traditional features, seems to have been the first to link the promised blessings of the
future firmly to the progress of science, not just as a source of material
benefits, but as providing in its devotees a new and more exalted type
of human being. He does not lack followers.

Secular faiths

Marxism and evolutionism, the two great secular faiths of our day,
display all these religious-looking features. They have also, like the
great religions and unlike more casual local faiths, large-scale, ambitious systems of thought, designed to articulate, defend and justify
their ideas – in short, ideologies. Is there still some plain, simple mark
by which we can establish their non-religious character? This really is
not so easy a question as it may look. It is certainly not enough to say
that they do not involve belief in God. Taoism does not do this either,
not does Buddhism in its original form. And the question whether the

Buddha is now 'a god' is not a simple one at all. He is, after all, to be sought and found within us. Moreover, where there are 'gods', their nature varies enormously. They certainly need not be creators. The world is often held to be timeless, or to have some other origin. Neither, on the other hand, does religion necessarily involve the immortality of the soul. Judaism in its early form does not seem to have involved human survival after death. Even for Buddhism, the soul will eventually be dispersed into its elements. And so on.

The reason why it seems worth while to refuse to draw a firm line here, and to go on considering these borderline areas impartially, is that where religious elements arise outside their familiar limits, we are liable to miss the special shapes which they contribute to the systems they affect. For this reason, I think that to say that Marxism or evolutionism, or indeed art or science, is serving as a religion, can be a useful way of speaking today. It is not like saying that golf is someone's religion, which is probably just a joke, and at most means only that it is the most important thing in his life, the thing to which the rest gives place. Here there is not likely to be any system of thought arguing that golf ought to take precedence, and giving reasons why it should do so. Moreover, devotion to golf is likely to have only a negative effect on those parts of life which take place off the golf-course. It leads to their being neglected, not to their being differently conducted. But the other candidates we are now considering do have those thought-systems and that wider impact. They are, not accidentally but by their very nature, dominant creeds, explicit faiths by which people live and to which they try to convert others. They tend to alter the world.

What is the general standing of such secular faiths? When they first began to appear in the nineteenth century, they had an obvious attraction for idealistic people because they were not then tainted by any such grim record of political misuses as they attached to Christianity. By now we know their black possibilities better. But their appeal, which rests on their power to make sense of a threatening and chaotic world by dramatizing it, has certainly not grown less. That makes them more frightening still. What is to be done about them?

Academic thought has in general responded to them suspiciously but negatively, by territorial arguments designed to rule them out of its province. From the philosophical end, the notion of a 'naturalistic fallacy' or supposed logical flaw invalidating all argument from facts to values was thought to explode them. From the factual end, the other half of the drawbridge was pulled in. Positivists deliberately narrowed the notion of 'science' to mean only the establishment of particular facts through experiment, excluding the wider thinking out of which the general questions arose. Karl Popper's rather extreme and simple negative version of this view, in which even the establishing of a fact dwindled to the more modest falsification of a particular hypothesis and theories to collections of facts, became an orthodoxy among scientists eager to defend their territory against invasion by non-specialist thinkers.[4] But this ruling, as well as the corresponding one about moral philosophy, was quite unrealistically wide. Cut off like this from the main body of thought, neither study makes much sense.

The interconnectedness of facts and values

Neither facts nor values can be properly conceived in this drastic isolation from each other and from the central conceptual area which connects them. At the scientific end, this became clear as soon as Thomas Kuhn drew attention to the mass of very complex conceptual apparatus which needed to be used and taken for granted if anybody was even to start framing scientific hypotheses.[5] Science is not just a formless mass of experimental data; it is a system of thought in which they are ranged, a system which connects with the rest of our thinking. Equally at the ethical end, as soon as the euphoria produced by the prospect of barring thought from morals had passed off, it grew clear that the idea of completely abstract 'values' conferred by arbitrary choice was an unreal one. We can value things only in a context which makes our valuing intelligible. And this valuing is not just a flat vote for or against them, a general ruling that they are good or bad. It is always a much more specific response – a response appropriate to some particular quality, to (say) a certain kind of meanness or generosity, fairness or unfairness, kindness or brutality.[6] These qualities in their turn are not just arbitrarily connected with the situations they belong to. Though there are borderline cases – as there are with other qualities – there are also always central, typical ones; cases which we would naturally cite if we wanted to explain the very notion of these qualities – cases where we quite properly ask 'what on earth would you count as meanness or brutality if not this?' Certainly the word that we use, and the special thought that goes with it, belongs to our own culture, and the general capacity for the reaction it expresses belongs to our species. But this does not make them arbitrary. It is not an arbitrary fact about any of us that we belong to the culture and to the species that we do. That is part of our proper description. We are not just standard, abstract minds, tossed by chance or malice on to a strange planet. We are not even visitors from Betelgeuse. We are therefore not the aliens and gypsies that Jacques Monod calls us, but natives. Our history and biology, which locate us here, ensure that by the time we are called upon to do any valuing the facts of this planet have plenty of meaning for us. They fall within a system. Through it, we do our moral thinking. Monod's isolationist position must be examined more fully later (in chapters 9–11). It has been immensely influential, not just because he was a highly distinguished molecular biologist, but because he put his finger on certain very painful anomalies in current notions about the function of science, and supplied medicines for them which have been widely accepted. As will become clear, I believe that these are only palliatives, concealing the true nature of the complaint, and that a much fuller diagnosis is needed.

For the moment, however, we are dealing with that aspect of moral scepticism which is grounded in philosophy – with the contention that thought concerns itself only with facts, leaving values to be dealt with by feeling, or by some kind of inarticulate decision in which the intellect is useless. That we are not helpless and inarticulate in this way becomes obvious on the many occasions when that thinking goes wrong – when we fall into moral difficulties and confusions. Faced (for instance) with a clash between two cultures, or between justice and mercy, or between honesty and kindness, we do not just toss up. We do not treat the issue as an arbitrary one, like having to choose between two unknown restaurants for our dinner. We continue, however weakly and blunderingly, the kind of work which has built up our standards in the first place. We go on thinking. Arguments about this kind of problem fill our literature, and constantly increase our insights. The rules for conducting them are quite as complex as those of scientific reasoning, though naturally quite different.

Neither in science nor in morals is it easy to find cases of perfect, irrefutable reasoning on difficult subjects. But in both it is quite easy to find cases of bad reasoning and to say roughly why they are bad and what sort of thing needs to be done to make them better. In this way we develop a range of better and worse cases, and gradually work out the standards which underlie that range. In moral questions – and indeed in all practical questions – changing circumstances continually alter the problems, which does make work on them more difficult than it is in science. But that is quite another thing from making it impossible. Faced with a dilemma, we do not expect an infallible oracle. What we do is to look for the central considerations on both sides, and for the main outlines of a conceptual scheme which will enable us to weigh them against each other. This is enough to get us started. If we do not have this much material for a world-picture, we shall be paralysed for ordinary practical dilemmas as well as for moral ones, and our life will grind to a halt. If we do have it, we can start work, groping outwards till we find more and more connections which light up the subject more fully. In this way, communal conceptual schemes are forged, by which we can carry on moral business. Though they are always inadequate and constantly need change or correction, they are workable. Without them, more ambitious schemes could never get started. They supply the models and standards for all the more abstract, limited, specialized, artificial ways of thinking which we patent for particular purposes in special branches of study. It is not inside any of these special branches, but in the outside, rougher, more general intellectual region, as sharply excluded from 'anti-naturalist' philosophy as from Popperian science, that we shall have to work if we want to make some sense of ideologies – or indeed, more widely, to understand the various elements in the notions of *science* and *religion* and how they are related. This is not a region outside all systematic enquiry. Much worse, it is one where disciplines overlap and none quite fits, where we need more than one kind of language and more than one kind of method. Whose business is it? Where is its specialist? A word must be said about this in the next chapter.

3
Demarcation disputes _____

Cursed be he that removeth his neighbour's landmark.
Book of Common Prayer

Better and worse faiths

We need, then, to start by resisting unrealistic scepticism. We do have this general capacity for making sense of our moral ideas and for explaining our judgments to one another. We are therefore not actually helpless when it comes to evaluating faiths and ideologies. We can, for instance, separate the various elements in a faith and approve of some of them while disapproving of others. And for this we can give our reasons. We are not reduced to the mere legalistic manoeuvre of outlawing them wholesale from learned life by saying that they are not science. Most of human thought which has a practical bearing is not science either. This does not place it beyond criticism. Most moral thinking, in fact, deals in some way with connections between facts and values. That can be done well or badly. What is wrong with bad ideologies is not that they are trying to do something of this kind, but that they are doing it wrong. Their selection both of facts and of values is a bad one, leading to distortions at both ends.

If, therefore, we want to pin down what is wrong with each of them, we need to survey its field as a whole. In order to distinguish bad faiths from the more reputable ones just mentioned – from faith in humanity, say, or in democracy or art or science – we have to take their arguments seriously and locate their faults. We cannot just dismiss them in advance because they lie outside science. The arguments for our own faiths, including faith in science itself, lie outside science too. If we have the impression that our own faith needs no argument, being simply self-evident, this is merely a dogmatic slumber. We are resting on the laurels of those who, in the past, have with great controversial effort established the value of what we now take for granted. In the case of democracy, we are profiting from the stupendous spadework of the Athenians and the great Enlightenment thinkers. In the case of science, we owe a lot to Aristotle, but the immense depth of modern veneration and confidence, centring above all on physics, comes from Descartes. If any of us were now called upon to do this work again for ourselves, arguing to convince someone from another planet or culture, we would be in deep trouble. We do not encompass all these arguments, any more than even the most comprehensive scientist encompasses all the arguments of the neighbouring specialities on which his own must rely. Faith in the institution as a whole, and in most of its practitioners, is a necessity.

But this does not mean that the arguments are not there. Once some central presupposition of the system is questioned, and we grasp the objection being made to it, we can take up the floorboards and see what is wrong. To do this, we must at once face the important question, *'for what* have you faith in this?' Most kinds of faith are specific and limited; they can be justified for certain purposes but not for others. It is right to have faith in a car as a means of transport, but not as a divinity. When we look consciously at the arguments by which we would need to justify a particular faith this usually becomes obvious. One kind of faith will, if expanded without limit, compete with another. The enterprise of justifying any given kind therefore leads almost inevitably into a general discussion of our different aims and the priorities among them. And this is a general philosophical topic. It is not an internal one to be settled by the faith which is trying to expand. Thus, people today who have a specially strong faith in science – expressed by speaking of the 'omnicompetence of science' and claiming that it is the sole legitimate intellectual method open to humanity – are not themselves merely talking science. They are stating a very bizarre position in metaphysics. They are out-Descartesing Descartes, who did indeed claim that physics was in some sense omnicompetent for understanding the physical world, but still thought it quite irrelevant to conscious subjects, and grasped the need to use other methods there. The claim that the *methods* of physics are everywhere appropriate cannot be justified by Descartes's position that what physics tells us about the physical world is the fullest and clearest truth about it. (Indeed, that position may quite sensibly be taken to mean that what we mean by 'the physical world' simply *is* the abstraction described by physics. The biological, chemical and historical worlds are then seen as distinct, non-competing abstractions.) Neither can the special claim for the methods of physics be justified from the position of modern physicalists – philosophers, operating a good deal more subtly than Descartes, who hold that the physical world is indeed the only real one and that there is no need to posit a separate soul. They see how wild it would be to take this as meaning that, at the level where we actually have to live and think, immensely abstract concepts such as those of physics could be usefully deployed at all, let alone replace all other concepts.[1] To argue in support of this strange claim its champions would need both a well worked-out, convincing set of examples and a quite new range of metaphysical arguments. This need itself seems enough to show that physical science is not in the required sense 'omnicompetent'. Nor is there the slightest need to expect that it should be. Inflated claims of this kind are never called for; they are irrelevant to the true point and dignity of an enquiry.

Vastness and specialization

When we investigate the claims of this or that faith or ideology, then, we do not do so in a vacuum. We need to consider its relation to the other central interests, institutions and belief-systems among which it operates, and relate its claims to theirs. The work is inescapably vast. It has become necessary, however, at a time when all academic enquiries are withdrawing their frontiers, when the trend to increased specialization is becoming accepted not just as a fact but as a gain, and when for the first time it is beginning to be accounted creditable for learned people to reject questions of burning general interest. Huxley's trap has closed on us. It is no accident, of course, that these contrary demands have coincided. The same wide increase of intellectual activity which has produced the specialization has also undermined traditional systems of belief, leaving room in each case for a dozen others to spring up in their place. Thus the area of difficulties is constantly expanding, just when those studying it have been called on, as a matter of professional pride, to give up the telescope for the microscope, and if possible the electron microscope at that.

It is not surprising that the first and most general reaction was a defensive withdrawal, a shutting of the academic gates on all vast and vulgar questions, an anathema on the Victorian tradition of trying to combine learning with wisdom. Sages went right out of fashion. This policy, however, turned out to have the distressing drawback that the excluded doctrines prospered on the treatment and simply acquired an intellectual élite of their own. There is far too large an educated public outside the universities today for any monopolistic ban to be effective. Accordingly, academics are now getting a more open attitude. They are tending to rely less on exclusion by ukase and becoming readier to try to understand the popular doctrines. But the difficulties of this enterprise remain immense. It is no use simply to become an uncritical convert, but neither will it help to remain sharply negative, merely pointing out the doctrines' obvious faults. To do any good, the critic must also see why the doctrine was invented in the first place, and why it has been welcomed. The vast questions which it answers badly have to be directly faced. Better answers must be given, even if it is obvious that they too are still thoroughly inadequate. This is not a field where academics can get that seductive icing on their cake – the sense of having put things absolutely right. It is not even one where the methods to be used are already fixed and familiar. Discipline is needed indeed, but it is the discipline appropriate to explorers. It involves a constant sensibility to changes of terrain, a readiness to alter one's methods and improvise new ones where they are needed, combined with the capacity to see when one has stumbled into the ancient and subtle civilization of another enquiry, and is making an ass of oneself if one fails to take advantage of the techniques the inhabitants have already developed.

It is because all this is so confusing – because the rules for controversy on these topics are so hard to grasp – that it seems worth while attending here to the sociobiology debate. This would certainly not be worth discussing here merely for the sake of its strictly scientific content, which is real but limited, and of interest only in the context of many larger questions about evolution. The importance of the debate lies in the way in which this scientific content has become entangled with certain influential and emotive views about the nature and destiny of our species, views of the kind which is still officially supposed to be kept out of scientific controversy. The position is one which is rather common today of warfare, not directly between academics and the outside public, but between two academic disciplines, each fired by moral and political ideologies extraneous to it and often not fully understood. The fervent opposition which the moral conflict generates makes it almost impossible to sort out the factual issues, and the larger questions which lie behind both cannot be seen at all till the smoke of the clash has somehow been dissipated. At the same time, each party tends to have the impression that it is still on academic ground, repelling a non-academic intrusion. Alien ideologies are strident and obvious; one's own are habitual and taken for granted. They seem academically respectable.

What sciences are

This difficulty is more serious in the physical sciences than it is in the social ones. For social scientists, faiths and ideologies are obviously proper business because they are part of the subject-matter. Social scientists, like historians, are called upon to discuss both influential systems of thought and the feelings which underlie them. In order to do this, they have to be aware of their own attitudes. The discipline of becoming conscious of these and relating them to those one is discussing is a recognized part of such work; people who fail in it constantly come under criticism. The defect is common but it is universally recognized. For physical scientists today, this is much less true. Although unspoken attitudes to what physical science ought to be are very powerful, not much of them is articulated. Officially the business of science is taken to be simple – the establishment of 'objective' facts which look the same to everybody. Attitudes must be irrelevant to it. Background presuppositions are therefore much less discussed than they used to be, and what discussion there is tends to be negative – devoted to excluding borderline areas from science.

The effect is to leave many of today's physical scientists rather unpractised in general thinking, and therefore somewhat naïve and undefended against superstitions which dress themselves up as science. Creationism, for instance, cuts no ice at all with humanists and social scientists. Nobody trained to think historically is in any danger of taking it seriously, least of all theologians. It makes its academic converts among chemists and physicists – sometimes, alarmingly enough, even among biologists. Equally, the attitudes which will most concern us in this book – faith in future superman-building, faith in the mysterious force of bloody-minded egoism, fatalistic faith in chance, and various sub-faiths accompanying these – owe their success to the making of scientific-sounding noises without serious substance. Their direct appeal is to people devoted to the glamour of physical science. This is a different group from that of scientists themselves, but unfortunately it overlaps with it quite widely. It covers a large and devout public, including many in the social sciences, who defer on principle to physical science as such, and suspect that, if they are not yet using its methods on any subject, they ought to be. The effect on that public of these quasi-scientific super-stitions, once any physical scientists take them up, can therefore be rather serious, and their strength is remarkable. The case most publicized so far – the resurgence of Social Darwinist egoism in sociobiological literature – is indeed an alarming one. Officially, sociobiological writers understand the objections to this view per-fectly. They rehearse familiar refutations of it with references to the naturalistic fallacy and the like; they treat Social Darwinism as obsolete. But because the intensely competitive attitude from which it originally sprang is still their own, because competition is what they live and breathe, because they are totally culture-bound and do not know that human life can proceed in any other way, they continue to project this picture on to the cosmos and to treat it as part of science.

It is probably a considerable misfortune for the English-speaking world that our word 'science' does not, like the German 'Wissenschaft' mean simply a learned enquiry generally, but the physical sciences in particular with a rather shaky annexe built on for other studies so far as they resemble these. Since the word 'scientific' remains a title of honour, the idea that there is something wrong when (say) anthropology or psychology fails to look like physics is still influential. Even biology is constantly finding itself out of line. Accordingly, social scientists have been rather willing to accept, as the price of admission to the fold, irrelevant standards held up to them from the physical side. In particular, they have often pursued a very powerful and confused notion of 'objectivity' as requiring, not just the avoidance of personal bias, but a refusal to talk or think *about* subjective factors at all. The word 'subjective' then becomes a simple term of abuse directed at any mention of thoughts or feelings, and the word 'objective' a potent compliment for any approach which ignores them. This policy produced extraordinary distortions in Watsonian behaviourist psychology, where the study of conscious subjects was supposed to be carried on 'objectively' – that is as if they were something quite different, namely lifeless physical objects.

There is now a considerable move away from this bizarre and unprofitable approach, though there is still a great deal of confusion about how close the methods of the different sciences ought to be. But an effect which remains with us is that the unaware and uncritical attitude to faiths and ideologies which was licensed for the physical sciences has infected social scientists too. Both J. B. Watson and his successor in the behaviourist tradition, B. F. Skinner, in preaching their colourful versions of behaviourism, took for granted that its studied neglect of subjective factors made it so obviously 'scientific' that it scarcely needed any other recommendation. Their own very peculiar and distinctive ideology was never brought properly into the open or called on to justify itself in the way which such very general doctrines need.

Paradigms and presuppositions

The fact that this and so many other attitudes, many of them very strange and certainly most of them mutually incompatible, have been taken for granted as 'scientific' and therefore self-evident by their various promoters surely makes it clear that more care is needed here. Either (one would say) scientists need, simply for their own work, to study controversial issues and methods which are not part of science, or the notion of science itself needs to be widened again to include them. Modern usage seems to make the second alternative rather difficult. It is very interesting that Thomas Kuhn, in pointing out the importance of the wider background concepts, firmly gave the name 'normal science' to the limited work which proceeds according to pre-set plans without raising new questions. In Kuhn's language, original thinking is an *abnormal* activity for scientists. This seems too depressed a viewpoint. No doubt it is true that the highly original thinking which produces a new and necessary paradigm is abnormal, because it is obviously rare. But what about the degree of awareness which is needed to understand properly the existing concepts, to notice aspects of them which are beginning to make trouble, and to spot the occasions when rank error is creeping in under their cloak? This – which should surely be normal activity for a scientist – is a skill which calls for some grasp of what the attitudes currently taken for granted are. It therefore demands an understanding of what they are *not* – of the possible alternatives to them and the reasons which might support those alternatives. It requires that current dogmas are not taken for granted as eternal and self-evident, but used as stages in a process carried on by fallible and constantly erring human beings. Current assumptions need to be made consciously, not treated as things already proved.

Considering the enormous emphasis laid at present on the import-ance of momentous scientific discoveries and the general high ex-pectations for the scientific future, this flexibility might not seem too much to ask for. But in fact it has proved difficult for such suggestions to be taken on board as anything but radically destructive. There is considerable resistance still to changing the seductive notion of 'modernity' which ruled early in this century and still does rule in many areas – a notion of a single dark past, described vaguely as 'medieval', due to be destroyed and give way once and for all to a 'modern' present which will be final and never need changing. Modern architecture is one dismal case of this strange delusion; successive modern scientific world-pictures have provided another. In theory, dogmatic propagandists for any one of such pictures are resigned to being overtaken one day by the next Nobel prize-winner who will change it. But they expect this to be a local operation, the supplying of new facts. What they naturally cannot envisage is the defect in their own general background thinking which will make a new approach necessary.

Kuhn called this background thinking a paradigm. This term has proved useful but tantalizing; there has been much dispute about how to fix its limits. This is not surprising. The term is essentially open-ended. What it covers ranges far outside the strict limits of science, covering everything that Collingwood so usefully called 'presuppositions'. And since there are not, as Collingwood supposed, any 'absolute presuppositions' – since everything involves something else – this takes us an indefinite distance into the realms of the motives and imagination. The example of the dramas linked to the idea of evolution surely makes this clear. If we are not prepared to criticize these imaginative frameworks directly in their own suitable terms, we do not stand a chance of getting the facts straight.

The proper role of scepticism

This by no means commits us to helpless scepticism; indeed, it is the only possible remedy for it. It is not that the whole controversy is an arbitrary social construction. There is a real, vast, factual issue about the origin and development of terrestrial life, a huge set of interlinked historical and scientific questions with right and wrong answers. Things did actually happen in some specific way or other, which human thought is powerless to change, and there are genuinely better or worse methods by which we can approach, or deviate from, a tolerably correct general account of the whole process, and of such parts of it as give us adequate data. We are not free to make it all up. But even where we have plenty of data, and still more where we are starved of them, the way in which we describe it does depend also on our own approach. And the meaning which we then give to our description, the implications which we find in it for the rest of life, the deeper message which we take it to hold, depends on this still more heavily. From these flow both practical principles and further factual beliefs. These things, unfortunately, are not marked off from a set of narrowly and indisputably scientific items by any helpful system of labelling. The terms and concepts used in sober, neutral areas often turn out to have other uses as well; indeed, much of their usefulness depends on their doing so, and thus suggesting wider applications. Attempts to avoid this by making all the terms technical, or expressing everything in equations, would only hamstring thought, and would not achieve their disinfecting purpose, since the emotional attitudes attached to ideas would still be there, and would only be harder to recognize if they were not betrayed, as they often are now, by language.

In recent years, sociologists of knowledge have been useful in pointing out this sort of trouble. The weakness of their work is its spasmodic exaggeration. They tend to talk sometimes as though the facts did not exist, as though spotting a motive behind a particular line of theory settled the question of its correctness, or somehow prevented that question from ever arising. The weakness of this kind of extreme relativism has been shown in many ways, notably and most simply through the question of whether such theories in the sociology of knowledge are themselves ordinary scientific theories, or are somehow exempt from their own scrutiny. I am not now peddling any such sweeping sceptical or relativistic enterprise. But I do want to introduce an element of moderate, selective scepticism, which will make us watch out for particular sources of error.

In particular, we need to avoid extending the confidence which is due to the central, well-established findings of the sciences to a vast area which has only an imaginative affinity with them, an area where only the name and trappings of 'science' are present. The attitude sometimes called 'scientism' – a general veneration for the idea of science, detached from any real understanding of its methods – is at present extremely powerful. In that attitude, the notion of the role which the scientist sees himself as playing is inextricably linked with a view of the cosmos. The role makes sense only within a given drama, and the feelings which shape the role are inevitably projected to provide it with a suitable background. Uncontrolled indulgence in the drama enslaves one to the myth. A good example of this is Ghiselin's story, quoted in chapter 1, that 'the economy of nature is competitive from beginning to end'. This, though presented as a scientific finding from which psychological truths can be deduced, has no basis in science. It is a piece of bogus, melodramatic, informal psychology projected both on to evolutionary theory and on to economics. The projection on to economics is the older, and does of course also have a political source, as sociologists of knowledge have pointed out, in nineteenth-century justifications of the excesses of unbridled commerce. But this does not exclude the source in individual feeling; it supplements it. The satisfaction of appearing in the role of unmasker, and the indulgence of aggressive feelings which this particular drama allows, centrally determine not only the language but the choice of theory.

In discussing the personal end of this interaction, I have naturally started from the idea of drama. For the cosmic end, it will be more natural to start from the idea of myth. The two will eventually converge. And I shall suggest that the myths involved are not distinct from each other, but combine to form something which can usefully be seen as a faith or even a religion. Not to complicate things unduly, I have made no attempt here to follow the investigation over the border into issues of religious thinking proper, and relate it to existing discussions of the nature of the various religions and what they have in common. I have tried to proceed somewhat in the spirit of that very great psychologist and empiricist philosopher, William James, considering this borderline area as containing some varieties of religious experience which are both striking in themselves and noteworthy now because they are practically influential. It seems to me very important that we should always be aware of such things.

4

The irresistible
escalator

When the unclean spirit is gone out of a man, he walketh
through dry places, seeking rest, and findeth none. Then he
saith; I will return into my house from whence I came out; and
when he is come, he findeth it empty, swept and garnished.
Then goeth he and taketh with himself seven other spirits more
wicked than himself, and they enter in and dwell there. And the
last state of that man is worse than the first.

St Matthew 12: 43–5

The kaleidoscope reshaken

Evolution, then, is the creation myth of our age. By telling us our
origins it shapes our views of what we are. It influences not just our
thought, but our feelings and actions too, in a way which goes far
beyond its official function as a biological theory. To call it a myth
does not of course mean that it is a false story. It means that it has
great symbolic power, which is independent of its truth. How far the
word 'religion' is appropriate to it will of course depend on the sense
we finally give to that very elastic word. In any case, however, it seems
worth while to notice the remarkable variety of elements which it
covers, and their present strange behaviour. While traditional Christianity held those elements together in an apparently changeless and
inevitable grouping, we did not notice how diverse they were. But now
that the violent changes of modern life have shaken them apart, they
are drifting about and cropping up in unexpected places. Ambiguity
of the same fruitful but dangerous kind affects the names of other
complex human concerns – names such as *morality*, *politics*, *art*, *sport*
and indeed *science*. This ambiguity is dangerous when we do not

properly understand it, when we treat these complex conceptual groupings as if they were plain, single ideas. Confusion gets worse when displaced elements migrate from one main grouping to another. And today, a surprising number of the elements which used to belong to traditional religion have regrouped themselves under the heading of science, mainly around the concept of evolution.

The first thing I want to do here is to draw attention to this phenomenon, an alarming one, surely, above all for those who hold that getting rid of religion is itself a prime aim of science. If the fungicide shares the vices of the fungus, something seems to have gone wrong. But the phenomenon is of wider interest than this to all of us. Why does it happen? Why is this kind of cosmic mythology so strong and so persistent? The simplest explanation, no doubt, would be mere force of habit, the still-surviving toxic effect of Christian conditioning. But that is not a plausible story today. The days of really confident Christian education are simply too far behind us, and the leading myth-bearers are themselves too rebellious, too critical, too consciously and resolutely anti-Christian. If they are indeed the mental prisoners of their opponent, in an age when fashion is on their side and so much change is so easily accepted, there has to be a special reason for it. The power of these ideas still remains to be accounted for. This indeed is often somewhat uneasily recognized, but the explanations given for it tend to be crude and hasty. The matter is too important for this. We need very badly to understand the influences involved.

In trying to understand them we shall, I believe, do best if we detach ourselves as far as possible from the old Voltairean notion of a ding-dong battle between science and religion. Enquiring more calmly, we shall, I think, find that there is not one all-embracing reason why religious elements persist, but many distinct though related ones. Religion, like other complex human concerns, seems to be built up out of a wide set of natural tendencies which can be variously combined, so that it itself varies enormously in character according to the way in which we relate them. The same is true of science and also of art. Attempts to eliminate any such main grouping merely scatter its component tendencies in their crudest form to join other colonies. (Puritan attempts to get rid of art have shown this very plainly.) If we want to attack the evils infesting any special grouping, we need to look at it carefully to see just what its actual elements are at the time, and how far they necessarily go together. Classical Greek, for instance, had no word for 'religion' at all, and certainly arranged what we think of as its elements differently from how we do. Chinese, it seems, not only has no word for 'religion' but none for 'God' either, which causes difficulties for missionaries. It would be very short-sighted to suppose that this state of affairs flowed from an absence of what we call religion, and more enlightening to suggest that it meant a greater pervasiveness of it, whereby it was taken for granted all over the texture of life. The stark division of life into sacred and profane often posited in the west has not been attempted in China. Religion is less of a detached, specialized matter. Whatever the merits and demerits of this, it is probably important for us, and especially for those of us who distrust religion, not to suppose that current western definitions of it are necessarily the last word. This is specially important in connection with those definitions devised in the nineteenth-century positivist tradition to show religion as a childhood stage in the development of the human race, something which the west was rapidly outgrowing, though primitive peoples still unfortunately remained bogged down in it. More honest anthropology and history have made this tendentious, patronizing stance impossible today. We need a far more open mind. Perhaps indeed the concept of religion may be asked to look again at the Delphic inscription, 'know thyself'. But if so, the concept of science must certainly be asked to accompany it.

Pie in the future: prophecies and promises

We had better start by glancing at a few typical cases of the phenomenon in question: occasions when science appears to be stealing its supposed opponent's clothes. In this chapter I shall concentrate on prophecies, because they provide a specially clear example. It is a standard charge against religion that it panders to wish-fulfilment, consoling people for their present miseries by promising wonders in the future, thus dishonestly gaining support by dogmatic and unwarranted predictions. With this charge in mind, let us look at the concluding passage of an otherwise sober, serious and reputable book on the chemical origins of life on earth. The writer, a molecular biologist, having discussed evolution and described it, tendentiously but unemotionally, as a steady increase in intelligence, turns his attention to the future. Mankind, he says, is likely to throw up a new, distinct and more intelligent type, which will then become 'reproductively isolated'. He then goes on (and I have not cheated by removing any words like 'possibly' or 'perhaps'):

> He [man] will splinter into types of humans with differing mental faculties that will lead to diversification and separate species. From among these types, a new species, Omega man, will emerge either alone, in union with others, or with mechanical amplification to transcend to new dimensions of time and space beyond our comprehension – as much beyond our im-

agination as our world was to the emerging eucaryotes. . . . If evolution is to proceed through the line of man to a next higher form, there must exist within man's nature the making of Omega man. . . . Omega man's comprehension and participation in the dimensions of the supernatural is what man yearns for himself, but cannot have. It is reasonable to assume that man's intellect is not the ultimate, but merely represents a stage intermediate between the primates and Omega man. What comprehension and powers over Nature Omega man will command can only be suggested by man's image of the supernatural.[1]

Do any doubts arise? Just one. There may be a problem about timing. Major steps in evolution have been occurring at steadily decreasing intervals, and the next one may be due shortly. It must be the one the writer is waiting for. He adds: 'On such a shortened curve, conceivably Omega man could succeed man in fewer than 10,000 years.' Ordinary evolution, however, is too slow to allow of this startling development. So what is to be done? The reply comes briskly.

How then can Omega man arise in so short a time?

The answer is unavoidable.

Man will make him.

This is apparently a reference to genetic engineering, something specially important to those whose faith leans heavily on the dramatic idea of infallible, escalator-type evolution. They demand from that idea, not just an inspiring account of the past, but also hope for continued progress in the future. But the human race cannot be confidently expected to evolve further in a literal, biological sense. Human social arrangements, even in simple cultures, block normal natural selection. And the more elaborate they get, the more they do so. Nineteenth-century Social Darwinists attacked this problem with a meat-axe, calling for deliberate eugenic selection and harsh commercial competition, so that the race could go back to being properly weeded and could continue to progress. As we now know, however, these schemes were not just odious but futile. The scale was wrong. Commercial competition has no tendency to affect reproduction. And as for 'positive eugenics', it is not possible to identify desirable genes nor to force people to breed for them. Even if it were, their spread would still be absurdly slow.

The natural conclusion is that such schemes should be dropped, that the human race must take itself as it is, with its well-known vast powers of cultural adaptation, and make the best of its existing capacities. But this thought is unbearable to those whose faith in life is pinned to the steady, continuing, upward escalator of biological evolution. 'If evolution is to proceed through the line of man to a next higher form', as Day puts it, there simply has to be another way. That wish, rather than the amazingly thin argument he produces about recurrent evolutionary steps, is evidently the ground of his confidence. This confidence itself is of course not new. In the 1930s, the geneticist H. J. Muller made a very similar prediction:

> And so we foresee the history of life divided into three main phases. In the long preparatory phase it was the helpless creature of its environment, and natural selection gradually ground it into a human shape. In the second – our own short transitional phase – it reaches out at the immediate environment, shaking, shaping and grinding to suit the form, the requirements, the wishes, and the whims of man. And in the long third phase, it will reach down into the secret places of its own nature, and by aid of its ever-growing intelligence and co-operation, shape itself into an increasingly sublime creation – a being beside which the mythical divinities of the past will seem more and more ridiculous, and which setting its own marvellous inner powers against the brute Goliath of the suns and planets, challenges them to contest.[2]

The illicit escalator

This pattern, it should be noticed, is quite incompatible with regular Darwinian scientific theory. The idea of a vast escalator, proceeding steadily upwards from lifeless matter through plants and animals to man, and inevitably on to higher things, was coined by Lamarck and given currency by Herbert Spencer under his chosen name, 'evolution'. Darwin utterly distrusted the idea, which seemed to him a baseless piece of theorizing, and avoided the name. As far as he could see, he said, 'no innate tendency to progressive development exists. . . . It is curious how seldom writers define what they mean by progressive development.'[3] His theory of natural selection gives no ground for it and does not require it. As has been pointed out,[4] it arranges species in a radiating bush rather than on a ladder, accounting for all kinds of development, and also for some cases of unchangingness and of 'regression', equally as limited responses to particular environments. The notion of a ladder is of course derived from the older one of the stationary stair, the *scala naturae*, which combined some sensible ideas about increasing complexity with some far less sensible ones about hierarchy and government. No ladders are needed for classification. Linear development, or orthogenesis, is an idle fifth wheel to the coach. Darwin saw no reason to posit any law guaranteeing the continuation of any of the changes he noted, or to pick out any one of them, such as increase in intelligence, as the core of the whole proceeding. Spencer, by contrast, instantly saw a complicated law of increasing heterogeneity: to him, 'brief inspection made it manifest that the law held in the inorganic world, as in the organic and the superorganic'.[5] Accordingly, as one of his followers pointed out with pride, 'the Theory of Evolution dealing with the universe *as a whole*, from gas to genius, was formulated some months before the publication of the Darwin–Wallace paper' (a priority claim which Darwin never wanted to dispute).[6]

From that time to this, Spencer's bold, colourful and flattering picture of evolution has constantly prevailed over the more sober, difficult one of Darwin, not only in the public mind, but also surprisingly often in the minds of scientists who had reason to know its limitations. That distinguished physicist J. D. Bernal shaped it in a way which bears some relation to Day's in a remarkable Marxist Utopia published in 1929. Pointing out that things might get a trifle dull and unchallenging in the future, when the state had withered away after the triumph of the proletariat, Bernal predicted that only the dimmer minds would be content with this placid paradise. Accordingly, 'the aristocracy of scientific intelligence' would give rise to new developments and create a world run increasingly by scientific experts. Scientific institutions would gradually become the government and thus achieve 'a further stage of the Marxian hierarchy of domination'. The end result would be that scientists 'would emerge as a new species and leave humanity behind'.[7]

5
Choosing a world

What is not possible is not to choose.

J.–P. Sartre

Diverging human ideals

This scheme gives a clue to the meaning of Day's otherwise startling and mysterious prediction that the new superhumans would be 'reproductively isolated'. What made this idea seem conceivable was surely the already existing thought that scientists ought to form a caste apart, running the world without any possibility of interference by politicians, historians, voters or members of any other alien or intrusive group. This idea was strongly promoted by H. G. Wells, and was altogether rather popular in the inter-war years. It is still often found in science fiction, and permeates much other literature. Since a training in physical science does not of itself qualify people as administrators, the word 'science' tends to get a rather odd meaning here. It often seems to centre on membership of the club or tribe of scientists, and on rejection of other competing clubs or tribes, rather than on theories or even ways of enquiry. This usage is delightfully shown in B. F. Skinner's Utopia, *Walden Two*, which he repeatedly and devoutly claims is scientific. But the only sense in which this bizarre place could possibly be called scientific is that its founders think of themselves as scientists, that is, members of the laboratory-based tribe, united against e.g. historians. Their curious schemes are not based on discoveries or arguments drawn from any science, but on simple wish-fulfilment about ways of ordering life which would suit scientists. For instance, babies in Walden Two are brought up in almost total isolation and monotony in air-conditioned cells up to the age of a year, and still spend much of their time there until they are three. That treatment is so successful that thereafter they are perfectly adjusted members of society and their emotional development gives no further trouble. This, Skinner explains, is not just a good way of producing sane, balanced adults, but the only way. The founder of Walden Two can therefore fully excuse his own rather obvious emotional deficiencies by the agonized cry, 'Can't you see? I'm not a product of Walden Two!'[1]

It should be noticed that this story is directly contrary to a central tenet of Skinner's actual scientific beliefs – namely that since man has no instincts, behaviour can only be produced by other behaviour. Conditioning is essential. If that tenet is right, the children should come out of their cells even more stunted and helpless than the rest of us would expect – indeed, almost exactly as they went in. That they can come out in an admirable state of development is a miracle, explicable only by a far stronger theory of innate tendencies than those against which Skinner constantly fought. It is not a scientific dream. It is merely the dream of a shy, unsocial scientist.

Skinner, however, at least did not propose that his enlightened scientists should form a hereditary caste, reproductively isolated from the proles. After the Second World War, a certain embarrassment began to surround this kind of proposal, and for some time it was no longer openly supported. Instead, the emphasis was usually laid on simply increasing intelligence. But it seems clear that this is at least often seen as equivalent to the proposal to produce more and better scientists.

This interpretation seems the only possible explanation of the strange lack of interest in the problem of conflicting ideals. What sort of intelligence are we to aim for? Indeed, more basically still, why is intelligence as such to take precedence over all other human ideals? Such problems are bypassed entirely. Thus, the Nobel prize-winning molecular biologist J. Lederberg writes in *Towards Century 21*, 'Now what stops us making supermen? The main thing that stops us is that we don't know the biochemistry of the object that we are trying to produce.'[2] It does not seem to strike him, any more than Day, that we cannot identify or conceive that supposed object at all, because of the relation in which we stand to it. There is an immense range of human ideals. But a product which is to be manufactured must be specified exactly. Will Nietzsche's supermen do as a model for the Omega factory? or perhaps Bernard Shaw's Ancients? Do we want Super-einstein, Supernietzsche, Superbeethoven, Superconfucius, Super-darwin, Superbuddha, Supernapoleon, or some sort of highest common factor (designed by a committee) between these and all other human eminences? How are the superwomen to be fitted in? Even if we somehow made an arbitrary choice, the whole idea of the lesser designing the greater is surely incoherent. Could a child invent an adult, or a crook invent an honest person? Everybody projects their faults into their work, and the more ambitious the work, the more glaring the faults become. We see these limitations plainly when we look back at the past, or outward at other cultures. If each previous century had been given the chance to put its ideals in concrete form, to produce its own supermen, we know just what faults we should expect to find in the products.

Superman buffs today commonly hope to escape this kind of partiality by assuming: (1) that what is needed is simply more of a single, timeless abstraction, intelligence, measured by intelligence tests; and (2) that that abstraction is a genetically distinct characteristic, controlled by its own gene or genes. Both these ideas, however, are indefensible. Intelligence in this sense – cleverness – is certainly useful, but how it is used depends on the aims of those using it. Like other powers, it is just an added danger in bad hands. And clever people, simply as such, unfortunately do not show the slightest tendency to be either less wicked or less weak than stupid ones. What we normally mean by 'intelligence' is not just cleverness. It includes such things as imagination, sensibility, good sense and sane aims: things far too complex to appear in tests or to be genetically isolated. And even what intelligence testers mean by intelligence is itself just a convenient compromise – entity specially evolved for use in the social sciences – handy undoubtedly for many purposes, but not related to the biological complexity of nerves and brain, and a nonstarter as a possible distinct, genetically heritable characteristic. In *The Mismeasure of Man*[3] that very humane and shrewd palaeontologist Stephen Jay Gould has told with careful fairness the dismal story of the long attempts to treat it as such, and has made clear that their failure was not accidental, nor even due to distortion by sinister political motives. The scheme itself is incoherent, and without those political motives it would never have been entertained. Certainly we need our nerves and brain to think with. But the power of thought to which they contribute is not something which can be sliced off and packaged separately. It is not an ingredient to be measured out into the stew, but an aspect of the whole personality.

Utopia trouble

Does this dismissal sound unduly dogmatic and high-handed? It is, of course, extremely hard today to look clearly at questions about the possibility of such projects. On the one hand, because science has increased technical possibilities staggeringly in the last two centuries, eminent persons have again and again made asses of themselves by denying the possibility of things which were subsequently done. But, on the other hand, science itself commits us to a belief in natural laws which are independent of human will and which have not been passed for our benefit. It gives us no sort of guarantee that the world is so made as to ensure that everything we want can be done. Indeed, in such little matters as mortality and the eventual extinction of the species, it hints pretty broadly that there are things we cannot have. The need to recognize the absence of this guarantee, and to come to terms with a universe which lacks it, is a central theme of this book. What I am opposing is the distortion of science itself to give either the guarantee or an illicit emotional compensation for its absence.

This is of course a much larger matter than the objections just made to relying on genetic engineering for human salvation. But people do tend at present to meet the large point by drawing a series of blank cheques on the future to meet the small ones. Is my pessimism here just one more fallible prediction about a local supposed impossibility, like earlier pessimistic predictions about flight? Can the continued development of the sciences be relied on to get us Omega man in the end?

Now of course it is true that the more technical set of objections – the ones aimed against supposing it possible to control reliably the change of human character traits by genetic tinkering – do depend on the state of genetics as it is understood today. These engineering proposals would look much more plausible if one used the 'beanbag genetics' of fifty years ago. And as it is true that nobody knows what the genetics of the future will be like, there could be a reversal. In the same way, when we say that time travel is impossible, or that there will never be perpetual motion machines or matter duplicators or the transmutation of other metals into gold, we are speaking in terms of physics as we know it. Some day our denials might look silly. But in choosing now between schemes for further development, we really have no alternative to using the ideas at present available to us. That is why the Patent Office will not now look at perpetual-motion machines.

The other objections I am making to the project – the ones concerned with the incoherence of supposing that we understand our own nature well enough to set it right directly, by choosing certain character changes, without first dealing with the value conflicts which at present tear the world apart – are independent of this technical issue. Naturally they too use current thinking, which may one day be altered. But however much one may expect this, it is unfortunately not possible to conduct an argument by simply sitting back and waiting for the other person's ideas to become obsolete. They have to be answered today, and in more or less the same terms in which they were stated, unless one can at once improve these. This kind of objection to the genetic approach does not depend on technical developments, for which we might have to wait, but on the whole shape of the moral and psychological problem to be solved. The libertarian political philosopher Robert Nozick states it well, in his general polemic against Utopias:

> Given the enormous complexity of man, his many desires, aspirations, impulses, talents, mistakes, loves, sillinesses, given the *thickness* of his intertwined and interrelated levels, facets, relationships (compare the thinness of the social scientists' description of man to that of the novelists'), and given the complexity of interpersonal institutions and relationships, and the complexity of co-ordination of the actions of many people, it is enormously unlikely that, even if there were one ideal pattern for society, it could be arrived at in this *a priori* (relative to current knowledge) fashion. And even supposing that some great genius *did* come along with the blueprint, who could have confidence that it could work out well?[4]

He adds the comment of another political philosopher, Alexander Gray, that 'no Utopia has ever been described in which any sane man would on any conditions consent to live, if he could possibly escape' which is true enough. But unless the expected Utopia had first been fully thought out *as a whole*, the designing of citizens for it could never be started. These people would not be, as most technological products are, tools to be used for a pre-set purpose belonging to their users and designers. They would need to be the owners of entirely new sets of purposes, and parts of a social whole quite inconceivable to those who designed them. They would need to be solvers of enormous problems about the ways in which human beings are to live together – problems which we ourselves have not solved and do not even know how to state properly. If the genetic enterprise was to be worth while, they would have to approach these from a quite new angle. But for us to program them, we should need already to know what that angle was, to have cracked the nut ourselves. The scheme, in short, has all the snags of other Utopias, with the additional drawback of not showing its working, not making explicit the distinctive ideas and institutions by which it means to solve the age-old problems of human social life. Promising us genetic mechanisms will no more fill this gap than recommending an electric oven will show us how to cook.

Boring limitations

On the whole these wider conceptual objections to the possibility of making particular changes seem both more serious and more interesting than the more detailed and technical ones. Nevertheless, I think it will be worth while to pay some attention to these, because it is really interesting to see how strong a detailed mythology has grown up to make the idea of such operations look much more plausible than it is. It is clear from a number of popular books, such as *What Sort of People Should There Be?* by the moral philosopher Jonathan Glover,[5] that the DNA is often conceived as something like a film-strip, which can be unrolled and examined. The frame depicting a particular characteristic can then be directly spotted and any necessary changes made, so that the resulting picture now conforms to our wishes, without any interference with the rest of the film. No doubt scientists have not meant to convey this wild story, but a number of commonly used metaphors tend to produce it, notably the description of genes as 'coding' for particular characteristics. In this metaphor, the 'reader' of the coding is of course the organism itself, which is thus moved to produce what is needed. To the uninstructed human reader, however, it sounds as if the scientist could read the code, as he might read a film-strip. Next, there is a systematic distortion of language in the frequent talk of genes as 'coding for' behaviour, as if a given gene produced a given unit of behaviour, independent of all experience, as infallibly as it might produce brown eyes. That very shrewd ethologist, Patrick Bateson, in a recent review, tells the significant story of how he took a colleague to task for using this language in an otherwise excellent article on the genetic analysis of behaviour:

> I said 'You can't mean that genes bear any straightforward correspondence to behaviour' and I began to give him a lecture on the systems character of development. He listened quietly and replied disarmingly, 'You are right. The trouble is I can't think like that.'[6]

The incapacity is common, and the temptation to oversimplify such processes is enormous, not least when there are computers to be programmed. In this way, scientists who themselves know better can mislead not only the defenceless general public including their students, but eventually themselves as well.

Let us then glance quickly at a few of the practical obstacles to this sort of scheme. The most plausible cases where such techniques are proposed for humans concern the elimination of certain inherited conditions producing diseases. These cases (whatever other difficulties they may turn out to involve) share two exceptional advantages with certain simple physical characteristics like eye colour. First, they are clearly identifiable; there is no controversy about who is a haemophiliac. It is therefore possible to learn something about their genetic pattern directly from family history. Second, they are, so far as is known, governed by a single gene.

This situation is exceptional. Many qualities are present more or less, and are affected both in their degree and their kind by a great number of factors during the individual's life as well as in his genetic make-up. They cannot be firmly identified, and with humans, where culture is such a powerful factor, family history would tell us next to nothing about their genetic basis. Moreover, even where that basis is at work, each is not normally tied to a single gene.

Most properties are affected by many genes; most genes affect many properties.[7] Also, owing to polymorphism, properties which are similar in living individuals may be produced by different combinations of genes. The effect of a given gene can vary greatly, too, according to the influence of other genes which are combined with it. Moreover, genes tend to be correlated in blocks in a way which usually makes it hard to identify the influence of each of them. Thus, even properties which might seem no more complex than eye colour are normally impossible to change without a large, unpredictable series of other changes. But the qualities we might want to produce (putting aside for the moment the crushing difficulty of deciding which of them to favour) could not possibly be ones as simple as eye colour. Intelligence for instance – which may seem to be one of the simplest of them – is known to have a very complex physiological basis, with the two brain hemispheres contributing in extremely subtle ways and undoubtedly other parts of the nervous and glandular system playing unknown parts. It is not, therefore, just a matter of finding which genes control some one quality, and checking what other effects those genes have, but of finding a whole range of interlinked qualities, each controlled by its own indefinite complexity of genes.

The experimentation problem

If anyone still feels like treating all this as simply a long task, to be dealt with by persistent experimentation, it is time to ask just how that experimentation would be carried out. Will it be by consent, and if so, whose consent? And how long is it supposed to take?

If some extraterrestrial being were to become interested in the inherited element in human behavioural tendencies, and wanted to experiment on its genetic basis, the first precaution he would need to take would be to have a life-span about as much longer than ours as ours is longer than that of bacteria, or at least of fruit-flies. Otherwise he would not live to see the result of his work and – supposing science on his native planet to go on much as it does here – ideas would have changed so much before anybody did see it that it would no longer be of much interest. The second precaution of course would be the one which is also taken with bacteria: not to ask his subjects what they wanted, but to decide flatly on certain changes, chosen simply for their genetic convenience, and to pursue them regardless of anyone's views except his own. He would have to start with a long exploratory programme of controlled breeding, simply to find out how desirable traits were linked to genes in the first place. Supposing that this did eventually begin to show some hopeful pointers, there would then have to be an equally long phase of trial-and-error breeding to check his hypothesis. On what terms is it expected that human parents would consent to let themselves and their children be subjects for this prolonged and quite unpredictable process, from which they could expect nothing but harm?

It is rather extraordinary how advocates of genetic engineering overlook this problem. Thus Jonathan Glover, in a discussion notable for its carefully calm tone, says this:

> Any program of genetic engineering to modify our intellectual functions would obviously have to be very cautious and experimental. But *once it showed signs of working without bad side-effects*, it seems likely that some parents would choose to have children who would transcend our traditional limitations.[8]

So who were the experimental subjects up till then? Glover, who is not actually one to propose using the proles, is probably thinking that they can be animals. The corrupting effect of habitually treating animals as expendable confuses people's thought here, but this is no solution. Human genes are what is in question, and no work would be the slightest use that was not done on a human subject. The familiar difficulty about medical experimentation comes in, but in an extreme form.

What the experimental subjects would get would not be a risky but promising prospect of cure, to which they might consent if they were ill enough, or benevolent enough towards future sufferers to want to contribute to knowledge of their illness. Instead, it would be a gratuitously twisted constitution, an unguided tampering with the only set of capacities which they have for their life-time. Of course there is an off-chance that it might work out well. But at the outset there is absolutely no reason to expect this. Just as most mutations are harmful, it is to be expected that most interferences with a very complex genetic program would be so at first, since they would be nearly as blind as mutations. As for consent, the person most concerned could not possibly give it. The parents could, but why on earth should they be willing to?

So desperate is this dilemma that it might not seem possible to make it worse, but Glover does so. Replying to the objection that relevant human qualities, such as aggression, may not be under much genetic control anyway, he says that this is irrelevant, since:

> all this would show is that, within our species, the distribution of genes relevant to aggression is very uniform. It would show nothing about the likely effects on aggression if we use genetic engineering *to give people a different set of genes from those that they now have.*[9]

What does this extraordinary phrase mean? It presumably cannot mean an entire new set, like false teeth. It most plausibly means either the introduction of some anti-aggressive genes never found in humans before (from where? how made?) or the thorough rearrangement of existing genes in such a way as to suppress those currently held to produce aggression. (It is taken for granted that less aggression is what is needed.) Both these proposals are so drastic as to increase the experimentation problem enormously. No one could have the least idea how the attempts might turn out. There is another snag, however, which is cognitive rather than moral, but no less disastrous. It would be necessary to establish how successful the changes being attempted were. How could this be done? The job of controlling aggression is done, as things are, by many cultural means. These are constantly changing, and affect each individual differently. Suppose an improvement took place, how is the environment to be discounted? Even if the experimental seedlings showed an average differential improvement, how could one be sure that this was not due to their experimental status and the special wish for improvement inspiring their parents? Control conditions are in principle impossible.

Because culture is known to have such power, it is not really possible for Glover to take the line he does of simply not being interested in enquiries to discover how far the qualities in question are genetically controlled at all. He dismisses these by rejecting claims to exactness, such as that aggression is 95 percent environmental. This is undoubtedly right; such figures are far too ambitious. But that does not get rid of the question of how much difference one could possibly expect to make by genetic means, and therefore how much effort it is worth directing to these attempts in proportion to other ways of sorting out human life. About aggression, too, another interesting problem arises. There already are quite a lot of people about who are markedly less aggressive than those around them. What happens is that they tend to get pushed around and to have less influence than they should on human life. It is not impossible for them to make their way by other means, but it is hard, especially in societies like ours which are rampantly competitive. To add other individuals, specially made, to this engaging band would not on the face of it have any general effect, since they would be put upon just like the existing members. Certainly it ought to be possible, in principle, for other qualities to be used to compensate for the absence of the cruder forms of aggression, both in individuals and in societies. But to expect to achieve this subtle aim directly by gross interference with an emotional constitution of which we have only the vaguest understanding seems wild.

Glover, who shows a good deal of sensibility to problems of this sort when he happens to notice them, remarks on some possible dangers flowing from our ignorance:

> A generation of parents might opt heavily for their children having physical or intellectual abilities and skills. We might leave out a sense of humour. Or we might not notice how important to us is some other quality such as emotional warmth. . . . Without really wanting to do so, we might stumble into producing people with a deep coldness. This possibility seems one of the worst imaginable.[10]

But this, and other disasters like it, are exactly the sort of outcome to be most expected from interference with this complex system. Nobody has the remotest idea what a sense of humour is, let alone what might be its genetic basis, or how to code for emotional warmth. Autistic children are, it seems, often highly intelligent; it is thoroughly obscure what is wrong with them, but it may well be genetic. There is almost certainly a whole range of possible disasters comparable to autism, which may be produced by the failure of combinations of genes which we now take for granted. In trying to produce increased scientific or musical powers – projects which Glover likes – we would indeed drive straight into the range of these conditions.

Is it fair to pile up this mass of rather down-to-earth objections against the Omega project, when it is so obviously meant as a sublime, far-reaching, straight-up-to-heaven one? Certainly this kind of response sometimes shows mere failure of imagination. Sublime proposals, simply as such, are entitled to some respect when so many of us do not raise our noses from our troughs at all. All the same, we do need somehow to distinguish between false and true sublimity. The trouble with the Omega project is that it is resolute about its physical means but much vaguer about its ends, and that when it becomes specific there too, it is (as we shall see) commonly much less convincing. And sublimity belongs to ends, not means.

But since it is the means on which we are asked to concentrate, doubts about their practicality do seem in order. When Omega-creation, or even any notable improvement in human nature, is put forward as a practical scheme and not just as an edifying story, it has two alarming features. The first, already stressed, is that its ideal aspect is so thinly developed. It simply slots recent biochemical discoveries directly on to existing Utopian fantasies without indicating any particular solution to the endless moral, political and practical problems which infest the ground between. It manufactures ideal people before even glancing at the thicket of confusions between inadequately related ideals which have so far seemed to make it impossible even to see how to conceive of them. It shows that rather dubious Nietzschean virtue: 'love of the remotest' – a penchant for long voyages as such, without any particular interest in their direction – and a contempt for existing people, excused by a somewhat theoretical attachment to people who are not here yet: 'Higher than love of one's neighbour is love for the remote and for the future. And I hold love for things and phantoms higher than love for men.'[11] There is a point in this sort of thing as a corrective, but it scarcely makes sense on its own. We will look further into this trouble in the next chapter.

The other matter, though smaller in a way, is also significant. The fact that so ostentatiously forward-looking a proposal makes use of out-of-date genetics cannot really be sneezed away. True though it may be that these theories might come back into fashion, just as perpetual-motion physics or the transmutation of metals might, the thing needs explanation. The central point, which we will consider more fully later, is that early in this century genes were considered as operating separately and independently, but they are now known to form a most complex system of interdependent parts. Even the word 'gene' is not the name of a single bead on a string; it is used to cover at least three different lengths of the continuous DNA molecule.

Unluckily, however, the symbolism attending the earlier picture was potent, and has kept it active as an underlying image which works, like the Lamarckian escalator, to distort people's thinking. About the proposals we are now considering, it has the obvious attraction of making schemes go on looking possible which on current ideas cannot possibly be so. It extends the euphoria which may have been excusable in Muller to support further fantasy in an age which can by no means afford it. But it has also a deeper, more purely imaginative attraction. Simply as an image, this idea of independent, disconnected genes supplies a seductive picture of a totally individualistic society. The atomistic notion of freedom as total detachment is figured in it alluringly, and power fantasies linked to this dream of irresponsibility are eagerly celebrated. Its most obvious incarnation is Richard Dawkins's book *The Selfish Gene*,[12] but we shall find it flourishing in many other places. At present all that is needed is to mention it, in order to point out that questions about the genetics of Omega-creation are not a mere pettifogging irrelevance.

6
The problem of direction

Then said Evangelist, 'If this be thy condition, wherefore standest thou still?' He answered, 'Because I know not whither to go.'

John Bunyan

The claim to momentousness

To light up the difficulties further, it will be worth while taking a further look at Jonathan Glover's tantalizingly titled book, *What Sort of People Should There Be?*.[1]

Glover's discussion is interesting because his tone and official intention are so different from the naïve, evangelistic Utopianism we have just been seeing. But at root I think he is just as machine-struck, just as carried away on a wave of undiagnosed faith in technology as such. On the surface he is highly moderate and reasonable. He quotes Muller's prophecies with suitable contempt, commenting that 'the case for genetic engineering is not helped by adopting the tones of a mad scientist in a horror film.' His declared aim is not to transform the human race according to a blueprint but to increase its freedom by allowing it certain valuable kinds of development which would otherwise be closed to it. He notes the difficulty of deciding who is to be in charge, warns us of the twin dangers of totalitarian, state-organized transformation and of anarchic, unbalanced changes produced by free enterprise in the 'genetic supermarket' so amazingly proposed by Robert Nozick. He does not, however, seem to notice the idiocy of this proposal. Nozick, while rejecting a genetically engineered Utopia on the grounds mentioned earlier, advises such a market 'meeting the individual specifications (within certain moral limits) of prospective parents'[2] as a means to securing a wide and varied spread of future types, and also as an expression of the parents' freedom. There being no point on which parents are so reliably conventional as their hopes for their children, what this would presumably bring about would be a society solidly manufactured for the demands of the previous age, and a gene pool needing to be altered radically in each generation by a set of people incapable of taking any other direction. All this supposing: (1) that it could work; (2) that the poisoning of parent–child relations which would follow on such open manipulation did not destroy family life altogether; and (3) that the choices offered were not in any case totally determined within a very narrow range by the scientists running the market.

Glover, however, accepts the scheme at Nozick's valuation and notes no danger but anarchy. All along, he gives the impression that the changes he expects from a moderate form of this scheme would be merely of the same order as those produced by new information technology or forms of transport. Yet, immediately after the passage just quoted, he writes:

> But behind the rhetoric is a serious point. If we decide on a positive program to change our nature, *this will be a central moment in our history*, and the transformation might be beneficial to a degree we can scarcely now imagine.[3]

And his main message certainly is that though we must act cautiously, we must on no account let this unique opportunity slip.

Why should this particular technology be expected to make a change which would count as a central moment in the history of the human race?

In answer, something must I think be said bluntly and generally for a start about the misleading effect of propaganda claims made on behalf of any line in learning or technology which has recently had some striking successes. Claimants here do not have to be dishonest, or more than usually obsessed by the need for research money, to be led on to exaggerate. There is a dazzlement, an unavoidable confusion of vision, which makes realistic foresight temporarily impossible. Molecular biology or biochemistry (if we may use the more convenient name) has been in this situation since the discovery of DNA. The world has seemed to be its oyster. It is neither accident nor some sinister prejudice on my part which accounts for the high proportion of quotations from biochemists in this book.

Resounding discoveries have combined with a sense of a commanding position on the frontiers of the physical and biological sciences to generate among these scientists a euphoric sense of cognitive omnipotence, of possessing methods which have been finally tested as correct and will be universally applicable. To many of them, their position appears to be that of missionaries from the physical sciences, spreading physical methods once for all over the hitherto recalcitrant realms of the life sciences, and thus over all remaining intellectual areas of the slightest interest. The great physicist David Bohm comments:

> Molecular biologists have discovered that in the growth and reproduction of cells, certain laws that can be given a mechanical form of description are satisfied (especially those having to do with DNA, RNA, the synthesis of proteins). From this, most of them have gone on to the conclusion that ultimately *all* aspects and sides of life will be explained in mechanical terms. But on what basis can this be said? . . . It should be recalled that at the end of the nineteenth century, physicists widely believed that classical physics gave the general outlines of a complete mechanical explanation of the universe. Since then, relativity and quantum mechanics have overturned such notions altogether. . . . Classical physics was swept aside and overturned. . . . Is it not likely that modern molecular biology will sooner or later undergo a similar fate? . . .
>
> The notion that present lines of thinking will continue to be validated indefinitely by experiment is just another article of faith, similar to that of the nineteenth-century physicists. . . . Is there not a kind of 'hubris' that seems rather often to penetrate the very fabric of scientific thought, and to capture the minds of scientists, whenever any particular scientific theory has been successful for some period of time? This takes the form of a fervently held belief that what has been discovered will continue to work indefinitely, ultimately to cover the whole of reality.[4]

Physicists, in fact, have abandoned the simple-minded mechanistic thinking which is the basis of biochemical superconfidence, and biochemists are liable to find themselves in the position of missionaries returning to Rome to find that a new pope has reversed the doctrines they were preaching. And though it is in a sense an accident that this has happened so soon, that superconfidence could not have endured long in any case. It is in the nature of science that such bold projections into the future always have to be modified.

Placing the need

So much, then, for the mere degree of euphoric confidence which is radiated, the general certainty of being able to make useful changes.

Besides this, if we are to speak of a central moment in human history, we would need another component, the sense of a special need, correctly located, which that technology and no other can satisfy.

Much more is needed here than the mere general belief, on which most of us would probably agree, that there is a terrible lot wrong with human nature. (Those who do not believe that there is such a thing as human nature at all will not be interested in genetic engineering to alter it in any case.) Any diagnosis which would show this technology to be relevant would have to fix what is wrong convincingly in a quality, or set of qualities, with a distinct genetic basis which could be changed, and say what changes were called for. Without that diagnosis, there is nothing momentous.

I find it remarkable that Glover's book does not deal at all in arguments about the nature of this need. Many of the changes he discusses are seen as relatively minor additions to the amenities and achievements of life: the production of musical prodigies, cleverer physicists or especially 'imaginative and creative' people. Others deal with alterations which seem equally slight (at least in Glover's view) but are distinguished by needing some sort of science-fiction device to bring them about, for instance the power to see directly into each other's thoughts at all times, or to switch off an unwelcome desire by some mechanical device. Here the writer is chiefly occupied with persuading us not to be too prejudiced against these (as he thinks) promising devices. But this overlooks the more obvious question: why these particular changes should be picked on. He claims that the first would make us more considerate and the second more autonomous. Neither story convinces me, but even if they did, it is hardly plausible that they would make all the difference needed for the salvation of the human race.

In general, the guiding aim which Glover sets up is increased variety to enrich human freedom, rather in the spirit of Nozick and of John Stuart Mill's *Essay on Liberty*. Mill said:

> As it is useful that while mankind is imperfect there should be different opinions, so it is that there should be different experiments of living; that free scope should be given to varieties of character, short of injury to others. . . . Human nature is not a machine to be built after a model, and set to do exactly the work prescribed for it, but a tree, which requires to grow and develop itself on all sides.[5]

Why, however, do we need genetic engineering to supply this many-sidedness, when we already have (as Mill pointed out) a bewilderingly wide range of options genetically provided, most of which we have never even glanced at owing to the narrowness and repressiveness of our cultures? In order to have reason to call in the engineers here, we would need reason to believe that human nature had failed us. Mill's whole book on Liberty is a celebration of human nature, a declaration of faith that it will *not* fail us. Glover's is the exact opposite, and the difference is crucial. To make Glover's remedies relevant, we would have to be convinced by good evidence that what holds back human achievement at present is lack of natural variety, that is, lack of talent. This seems a strange view, which would need a great deal of support. On the face of things, enormous potential for variety is already present, as is shown by the differences between people in different cultures, and the main thing that blocks our achievements is not lack of talent, which is running to waste all round us, but bad social arrangements and neurotic confusion in individuals. To commission more varied talents in that situation seems like pouring more good materials into a factory already choked by confusion and maladministration.

Even if it might be nice to have more musical prodigies, then, this sort of thing does not seem enough to constitute a central moment in human history. Nor does it at all answer the intriguing question of Glover's title, 'what sort of people should there be?' On this point he simply accepts existing notions. The questions about conflicting values which would seem primary if we are really discussing future directions for our society do not get raised at all.

The argument from untriedness

The obvious remaining issue, then, is the one which would perhaps be better titled 'what sort of people should there not be any longer, if we can possibly help it?' We turn away from the ambitious, optimistic perspective which sees the human race as an adequate going concern and boldly undertakes to make it far better, so much better that this will be a 'central moment' in its history. We drop the huge task which that perspective imposed of grappling with the mistakes of Plato, Thomas More, Jonathan Swift, Aldous Huxley and all the others who have tried to indicate right and wrong directions for humanity. We no longer undertake to supply a blueprint so much better than theirs that work on producing citizens suited to the new ideal can be put in hand at once. By a sudden *Gestalt* shift, we now stand face to face with the dangers which actually confront our species today. The question becomes much simpler. We are now looking for a 'central moment' in the sense of a turning-point which will remove the dangers and ensure survival. The task is now not constructive but remedial. Day's argument from faith in predestined future glory gives place to something apparently more realistic; an argument from despair. If, says

Glover, things are so bad that every known remedy is by now discredited, then it follows that an unknown one must be tried: 'Given our relative failure so far, we should at least consider the view that the abolition of war may need psychological changes which will not simply follow from political and social reform.'[6]

Which unknown remedy, however, does this argument favour? An indefinite number of willing physicians are equally entitled to use it for their own prescriptions. As it happens, B. F. Skinner made this idea a central plank of his platform in his book *Beyond Freedom and Dignity*. Dismissing all previous systems of thought as failures, Skinner observed:

> These have been around for centuries, and all we have to show for them is the state of the world to-day. . . . What we need is a technology of behaviour. We could solve our problems quickly enough if we could adjust the growth of the world's population as precisely as we adjust the course of a spaceship. . . . The fact that equally powerful instruments and methods are not available in the field of human behaviour is not an explanation; it is only part of the puzzle.[7]

The trouble, says Skinner, lies in our failure to assimilate our view of human behaviour fully and completely to the model of the physical sciences: 'Almost everyone attributes behaviour to intentions, purposes, aims and goals. . . . There is nothing like [this] in modern physics or most of biology, and that fact may well explain why a science and technology of behaviour has been so long delayed.'[8]

Skinner's remedy of course was not genetic engineering. He did not believe in any genetic causes of behaviour: he relied on behaviour modification through organized conditioning. His own argument could by now be turned against him; there is already enough experience at hand to show that behaviour modification is not the panacea we need. And he could reply, as people usually do, that it has never been properly tried. But this is just as true of the earlier ideas which he dismissed as discredited. The recommendation from untriedness is a vacuous one. It does not favour any new suggestion more than any other. Suggestions still have to compete on their own merits, and we have seen that the special claims of genetic engineering, on this basis, are not impressive. But also the accusation of 'having failed' is a stupid way of dismissing ideas. They are complex resources which nearly always have more in them than their previous owners have got out. Even the most drastic turning-points in thought always start from some existing notions and owe a great deal to them. Genetic engineering could not possibly be the totally new start which it is being hailed as, because the aims of the engineers would have to be exactly those they drew from the life and culture around them. And on the crucial question of *what* psychological changes are needed, they remain entirely vague and unoriginal. Apart from an increase in intelligence – which I have already suggested is irrelevant to our crisis because it deals with means and not with aims – the only ideas which get suggested are a decrease in aggression and an increase in altruism.

Aggression and altruism

The snag with both these is not only that, as just noticed, they seem bound to involve a loss of assertiveness and therefore of effective power for change. (The situation where a few remaining Stalins manipulate the docile hordes is a natural sequel.) But, more deeply, these simply are not distinct qualities which could be raised or lowered in isolation. The task is not at all like just putting less pepper in the stew. As for aggression (considered as a motive, not as the name of an offence), I would myself agree that it does have a genetic basis; there is even good evidence of a centre in the brain specifically concerned with it.[9] But, as with other such specialized brain centres, this in no way means that nothing else affects it, or that it somehow works alone. Such a 'basis' is not like the foundation of a free-standing pillar, but an organic part of a most complex system, the rest of our emotional constitution. Our capacity for anger and attack is deeply interwoven with our capacity for fear, for love, for respect and contempt, for grief, parent–child bonding, the attachment to home and an indefinite number of other emotional elements. To alter one of these would in all reasonable probability be to alter all. And in even trying to find what alteration we needed, we would confront the impossible task of separating aggression as it is conceived in our culture from the abstract possibility which underlies it as a human universal.

As for altruism, that is so general a term that it is hard to see what could possibly count as a single inherited trait underlying it. The most likely aim, if we are thinking of large-scale political matters like war, is to overcome the limitation of sympathies which usually restricts people's concern to those immediately around them. This is indeed the nub of the political problem. The difficulty in attempting to cure it has always been that it is relatively easy to curtail the limited sympathies which already exist – to make people ashamed of their undue attachment to those around them – but this does not necessarily have the effect of producing enlightened attention to those further off. Charity begins at home and tends to stay there. No adequate remedy for this has yet been found; we are still struggling with this barrier, knowing very well that the struggle is now for our life. But it is not the slightest use suggesting genetic engineering as a short cut. To be so, it would have had to identify just what it is that limits our sympathies and to show a way round it. Some might be tempted to suggest cloning admirably charitable people in the hope of getting a new race without narrowed sympathies. But this is to forget the effect of individual life and choice in the shaping of virtues. It is evident that upbringing does make an enormous difference here, though this knowledge does not help us as much as it should because we have a very uncertain grasp of the problems of upbringing. Still, this is something where we do have some hazy idea what we are about. Engineering for supercharity would not be like that; it is a realm of pure fantasy.

All these suggestions have the same attraction: simplicity. They look like ways to break the logjam with a single surgical intervention. But if there is one thing we know from the long and hard experience of the human race, it is that what is wrong is not simple. No doubt the trouble does stem from our emotional constitution. But the literatures and histories of the world are there to testify to how complex that is, and how hard to understand. It is not possible that 'science' in any form should now leap in with a solution, because the problems involved are ones which it has long carefully and explicitly excluded from its province. Even psychology, in its modern avatar as a science, has almost entirely turned its back on problems of motivation. It has tried to reduce them to behavioural regularities, and often been most unwilling even to think about their physiological basis. These problems have been left to psychoanalytic thinking, which itself was long excluded from the academic fold. Psychoanalysis has its own problems, including those arising from being often used as a secular faith. But it has made a very serious and persistent attempt to understand motivation without pretending that it is something else. And in none of its researches has it ever come across reason to conclude that the whole thing was really perfectly simple – requiring only the amputation or amplification of some simple emotional organ to straighten everything up. The position is not one where all that is needed is a scientific discovery which would make it possible to do that, even if such a discovery were a great deal more likely than my argument (based on current genetics) supposes. The difficulty we face is of an entirely different order. It involves the kind of understanding of human conduct which has been explicitly and carefully excluded from the whole concept of science as we know it today.

7
Scientist and superscientist

It is certain that men contract a general liking for those things which they have studied at great cost of time and intellect, and their proficiency in which has led to their becoming distinguished and successful. . . . That is why a criminal judge is an excellent witness against capital punishment, but a bad witness in its favour.

Charles Dickens, *Three Letters on Capital Punishment*, 1846

The wider interests of science

It cannot, then, be true that science itself demands that scientists should treat all problems as scientific problems. If the narrow definition of science currently used is to be kept, a great many problems of real scientific importance fall outside science. The construction of paradigms, and their relation to the rest of current thought, becomes a subject on its own. And when the pretension to Victorian sagehood was abandoned, all claim to resolve the more general problems of mankind officially went out of the window. Undoubtedly, however, this narrow definition is an unduly confining one. There is a much more natural, unofficial usage according to which science is simply what scientists do as part of their professional business. Since a great many of them are 'applied' – are agriculturalists, ecologists, government geologists or climatologists and so forth – this leads them quite naturally to count the social and political arrangements which concern them as part of their business, and to take the responsible attitude of people concerned with the effects of their purely theoretical work. And this kind of thing can happen at any time even with work which on the face of it is scientifically 'pure', as it did with atomic physics and the bomb. It would, I believe, be helpful if rather more attention were given to the positive advantages of making explicit one's wider 'scientific attitude' and to its unavoidable continuity with the other attitudes which shape one's life, even at times before these collisions have happened, with a view to being ready with some sort of a usable world-view when they do. And scientific education ought to make a great deal more provision for this.

As things are, however, what we have is an unnoticed oscillation between a very narrow view of science – useful for blocking arguments and shrugging off responsibilities – and a very wide one, useful for issuing unexplained demands in its name. In this wide sense, the interests of science as such have often been represented as calling for technological developments which could only be properly justified by social demands. Thus, over genetic engineering, Francis Crick, the much discussed and Nobel prize-winning co-discoverer of DNA, no less, sternly prophesies as follows: 'Provided mankind neither blows itself up nor completely fouls up the environment, *and is not overrun by rabid anti-science fanatics*, we can expect to see major efforts to improve the nature of man himself within the next ten thousand years' (my italics).[1] (The use of the word 'we' here is interesting.) But why should such opposition be 'anti-science'? In what way is 'science' committed to this project? The answer appears to be that Crick accepts the Lamarckian and Spencerian view of evolution as a firm principle of science, and sees it as predicting – nay, demanding – the continued upward development of the human species. Unless this is right, science, simply as such, gives no preference for this sort of investigation over the countless others which compose it at any moment. And as current scientific theories do not actually support this principle at all, Crick's cry remains totally unexplained.

Does he believe in the Spencerian prediction or not? On the face of things, the principle to which he is appealing looks rather like one which has commonly been seen as faulty both in Marxism and in the Gospel of St Matthew. It might be a matter of saving the face of science. Thus St Matthew often says that certain things were done 'that it might be fulfilled which was foretold by the prophets', and this is generally now thought not to be a very sensible aim. The idea of a duty to make a prediction come true is certainly an odd one.

If, however, avoiding this kind of appeal, we rest the case for superman-building on its own desirability, it must then compete on its merits with other proposed human schemes. When it does this, its most striking feature seems to be its irrelevance to all current, or reasonably predictable, human needs and problems. It is not going to arrest any of the shouting ills of the present. It is not the answer to world hunger or the arms race. But neither does it have the merit, which usually belongs to more remote ideals, of supplying a direction for our present conduct. Notions like perpetual peace or the brother-hood of man are real working ideals; they can change our conduct in the present even if we think them unattainable. But the idea of a superman-blueprint somewhere in the pipeline does not seem to have any possible moral application, except to demand resources and perhaps to make us shelve immediate problems in the hope that the superpeople will solve them. It is not an ideal at all but an expedient, and one which could not be put in hand until existing clashes of ideals had been resolved – a condition which itself probably presupposes the millennium.

Problem of the superfluous multitudes

Theodosius Dobzhansky, who holds a much more clear-headed, sensitive and humane variant of the same general faith in evolution towards better humans, is seriously worried by the thought that those of us outside the laboratories may not find that it gives our lives much meaning. He is at least aware that not everybody lives by the scientific ideal. He asks:

> Are the multitudes supererogatory? They may seem so, in view of the fact that the intellectual and spiritual advances are chiefly the works of elite minorities. To a large extent, they are due to an even smaller minority of individuals of genius. The destiny of a vast majority of humans is death or oblivion. Does this majority play any role in the evolutionary advancement of humanity?[2]

He concludes that actually it does, that 'we are not just manure in the soil in which are to grow the gorgeous flowers of elite culture', because 'it is imperative that there be a multitude of climbers. Otherwise the summit may not be reached by anybody. The individually lost and forgotten multitudes have not lived in vain, provided that they too made the effort to climb.' These are dismal metaphors, and moreover very strangely chosen. Why should we take the hasty journalist's angle on climbing and think none of it has any direct value except planting the flag on the last and highest peak? Fame is just a misleading spotlight; what climbers want is to climb. They work together. So do scientists; star systems and Nobel prizes distort what is happening. Again, the flower metaphor is strangely unbiological. Plants do not exist for the sake of their flowers any more than flowers for the sake of the plant. Again, death and eventual oblivion are the destiny of all, not just most humans. Nobel prize-winners are not exempt. This does not have to make anyone's life meaningless provided that he or she can feel part of something important which is being done. And that important thing need not be the later production of some startling object. It begins from the living of a satisfactory life by the group one belongs to, and the achieving there of whatever aims are currently most needed and valued. Of course it can extend more widely, and many feel an overpowering need to spread it so far that it does indeed conquer death. But this need for widening is not something which could be satisfied by pie in the future. Nobel prize-winners, even if they expect to help on the millennium by their work, are not necessarily specially fulfilled or satisfactory human beings and certainly not on a peak of human excellence of a different order from the non-prize-winning proles, condemned for ever to be valueless except as means. People, as Kant rightly said, are ends in themselves.

The situation of these proles is not in the end quite as black as this passage makes it sound, since Dobzhansky, signing up after some hesitation with the maverick Jewish palaeontologist Teilhard de Chardin for the prospect of a developing spiritual cosmos called the Nöosphere, eventually takes the final ideal to be, not the intellectual perfection of a separate caste, but brotherly love achieved by the whole human race. And brotherly love is something that can be immediately practised, not just planned as a biochemical possibility for others in the future. Nevertheless, the dismal limitations of an ideal which is both centred on a narrow set of intellectual faculties and placed entirely in the future are evident in the passage just quoted. In prophets like Day, they are a ruling factor, since the position of outsiders is not considered at all. The scientists can find fulfilment in framing the superman, for they mean to be inside the laboratory designing him, not only to their own specifications but in their own (improved) image. For them, self-worship is provided. But what anybody else could get out of it never emerges.

Professions, pygmies and personifications

Why does Dobzhansky even begin to get committed to this curious scientific elitism? Perhaps we should take stock here of which elements in these prophecies make it natural to reach for words like 'religious' in describing them. Speaking more generally about faiths (see p. 14), I suggested that their most notable characteristic was 'the sense of having one's place within a whole greater than oneself, one whose larger aims so enclose one's own and give them point that sacrifice for it can be entirely proper'. This whole has to be conceived as having its own aim or direction. In theory – say in a trade or profession – the aim might be thought of as just that wished by the people who now happen to compose the group, a chance combination like travellers who have agreed to hire a bus. Anyone can then get out at any minute, and, by voting, the remainder can change the bus's direction at will. This positivist account of group activities has its uses, but it does not do justice to the psychological realities. Social wholes in fact are almost always more than the sum of their parts, and can sometimes develop very remarkable independent characters and forces. They can add startling elements to the lives of those who compose them, and become very hard to control. Their dangers are well known, but their value for almost every important human activity is enormous. Even in quite unpretentious groups such as trades or professions, there is often a strong sense of a greater purpose transcending individual wishes, a purpose which carries everyone forward and which all must serve. This sense is not in the least superstitious. It merely acknowledges the remarkable part which joint, communal activity plays in our life.

How does this kind of thing relate to the situation of the pygmy who loves his forest, trusts it and says that it is his father and his mother? He too finds his place within a whole he did not make, and accepts its direction as giving point to his own. He certainly seems to be personalizing it, to be envisaging it as a superhuman being in a way in which (we would protest) western people are not when they talk of serving Science, or of doing what modern Medicine requires. The capital letters, we say firmly, do not put us in the position of meaning what the pygmy means, not even when we call for sacrifices of private interest to these entities and credit them with purposes transcending those of their group-members. Is the situation indeed totally different? I do not think it is half clear enough either what the pygmy means or what we mean on these occasions for this question to be dealt with briskly, and we must come back to it later. But what, meanwhile, about Muller and Day?

Their faith is placed, it seems, in three concentric entities – the scientific profession, the human race, and life or evolution. The direction of all three is the same and is set by the inmost one. It is towards ever-greater 'intelligence' in the sense of scientific achievement. Life is at times personified as the agent, and appears unmistakeably for Muller as a specially abrasive kind of interventive scientist – shaking, shaping and grinding. If this figure is the Life Force, by the way, it has greatly changed since the days of Bergson, Samuel Butler and George Bernard Shaw. Then it was female; it stood for the vast and mysterious natural fertility which mocked at human pretensions and especially at the absurd claims of abstract intellectual systems. Now it seems to have been chastened, and to have no subversive ideas to distract it from doing what scientists want.

The faith which Muller and Day have in these entities is by no means just the kind of faith which any of us might have in them for normal limited purposes. It views them as guaranteeing a most extraordinary future, one with no support in ordinary empirical scientific procedures. It expresses, in fact, a value-judgment – the judgment that scientific activity is particularly excellent and important – and credits that judgment to the creative force which it calls Life. Whether it views that force as personified is by no means clear. Theoretically no doubt it does not, but it is really not possible to make much sense of the notion of evolution's steady, careful progress towards this goal without language so deeply teleological that it implies an agent. Is the project really to attribute this purpose to physical matter as a whole – to treat it as an immanent, necessary, impersonal process – and is the personal language merely the effect of linguistic limitations? Perhaps it is, and if so, that is just the problem with which the more serious religions struggle. They do not think that their gods are just people either, but they have no other language to use. This will not separate Muller and Day from them. Any belief strong enough to support their startling predictions is faith, non-scientific faith, in an entity of notable supernatural powers.

What makes one unwilling to use the word 'religious' for this attitude is of course the shortage of awe and respect. Though the discoverers are treated with reverence, the force itself which has been discovered is mainly viewed as something to be used. As we shall see, this commonplace, exploitative attitude is by no means necessary for evolution-worshippers; it is very different from those of Dobzhansky and the two Huxleys. Day and Muller operate more like sorcerers; they propose to profit by the operation of this force and compel it to do their will. Nevertheless, Day at least does take it also as a guide, as in some sense the real owner of the purpose with which he identifies. He seems to be saying that the reason why we must actively press on with evolutionary business is that this simply is the enterprise of the universe, into which we are born. Though this view cannot be entirely disentangled from the mere prophecy that we shall do so, it is suggested by the tone. This idea, at once markedly less odious than Muller's approach and more shocking to contemporary humanistic thinking, is of great interest and will concern us again.

To sum up then:

1 The *belief* in future events does seem to be religious. It could not be scientific unless the escalator view of evolution had been duly established, and enough further evidence had accrued round it to support these startling predictions. None of this has happened.

2 Is there any *deity* involved, any supernatural creative being?

Officially no, but something called Life seems to be filling that role. References to it cannot really be taken as pure metaphor, because its function as unfailing planner is needed to guarantee that the future part of the escalator is solid and reliable. It is probably significant, too, for this issue about deities that both Day and Muller refer to traditional ideas of the supernatural, claiming them as mere fore-shadowings of what man in the future will actually be like: 'a being beside which the mythical divinities of the past will seem more and more ridiculous' as Muller joyfully observes. This is Nietzsche's move of substituting the Superman for God. The idea is that superstition has been avoided, because these people will be – one day – merely natural beings produced by earthly processes, but they are still so excellent that it is legitimate for us to get the satisfaction out of thinking about them which our unregenerate ancestors got out of imagining invented mythical figures. If, however, the prediction of their future existence is itself nothing but a myth, this superiority can scarcely be maintained.

3 Lastly, is there any characteristically *religious emotion*? There is not the awe, reverence and conviction of goodness which we in our own tradition think of as central. But there is certainly some sense of vastness and majesty ('whew' rather than 'lord I come') and also, with Day at least, a sense of directedness, an impression that the mere fact of belonging to this great process and recognizing it lays a duty on us to understand its aims and help to forward them. This sense, I have suggested, is characteristic of faith in general, and since in this case the faith is not just in a human group but in a non-human process or force, since the underlying belief is religious, it seems that the faith is religious too. It may be on the borderline between religion and magic, but that borderline is much wider and much less easy to diagnose than has sometimes been suggested. Sorcerers can sometimes take the forces they deal with very seriously indeed.

Second thoughts

So much for the general conceptual framework. About Day's *Genesis on Planet Earth*, however, a further postscript seems in order, because it has come out in a second edition with extremely interesting changes and non-changes.[3] Professor Lynn Margulis, herself an eminent molecular biologist and co-launcher with James Lovelock of the Gaia Hypothesis,[4] has noted the excellence of its scientific content and has supplied a foreword recommending it strongly as a textbook and explaining that it has been pruned of certain irrelevant naïveties which formerly spoilt it. It is no surprise, therefore, to find that the last chapter has gone, and that there is now no reference to Omega man or to genetic engineering. What is a surprise is to find what replaces these. This is a whole new chapter of prediction, now much vaguer but every bit as fervent, intense and evangelical, about the new levels to which mankind is just about to ascend. The argument from the diminishing intervals between earlier stages of evolution remains as confident as ever. There seems no suspicion that it could be unsafe to extrapolate a curve of development – if indeed this is one – without reference to conditions outside that curve. The argument is exactly like that which would prove that each of us will live to fourscore years, because that is what our developmental cycle dictates – except indeed that Day's is an argument from a single case, and one where our information is extremely scanty, since we know nothing of the development of any other biosphere and very little about our own. Most developmental curves end in a crash. Day does see the problems posed by the increasing energy consumption of higher forms of life. But since he is convinced that the progress will not stop, this only leads him to a more fervent admiration for the beings at hand who will surmount this obstacle:

> As happened with the eucaryotes, our potential will catapult us into a greater dimension. . . . Space is vacant, the lands are barren, inviting, like a repetition of that event at the dawn of the Cambrian. . . . The vastness of space holds us in awe and slowly pulls us towards it like an irresistible magnet. . . . And now the cycle is approaching a full turn. The procaryotes lost their preeminence not solely because they poisoned their environment but because they were on the edge of a larger dimension and created an energy potential that could propel a greater form of life into it. We too, stand poised on a springboard, surveying the direction of our future. . . . Machines are on the path toward self-sufficiency, like the biological cells. We may even build into them our consciousness and make them sufficiently independent that we inadvertently launch them on their own evolution. . . . Eventually man's role may be phased out and he will remain in an arrested state of development like the procaryotic microbe in his droplet universe, while his creation goes on to greater dimensions.[5]

Machine-worship – the cultivation of machines as an end in themselves and not as a means to something else – is a perversion which I cannot discuss fully here, though it probably has quite a lot to do with the obsessions we are dealing with. I have considered it elsewhere,[6] and I think that Erich Fromm was probably right to connect it firmly with necrophilia and the death-wish – with a preference for lifeless over living matter. What needs saying here, however, is that there is no scientific reason at all for Day's euphoria. The confidence in this particular developmental curve to do this job is entirely arbitrary. If indeed an evolutionary change is at hand, the most likely prediction by far is that it might be one involving the extinction of the human race. But, giving or taking a millennium or two, it seems wild to suppose that we are in any position to predict anything firmly about it. Again, however, Day certainly does not stand alone. He is exceptional only in his bold and open stance: others are often more cautious. But anyone who raises questions about beliefs of this kind will, I think, find that the responses they get confirm my own experience. This is the faith by which many people live.

One very striking fact about current expressions of it is that they are contriving to turn to their own purposes an idea which, on any reasonable interpretation, puts them out of business altogether – namely, the Gaia Hypothesis. This is the theory, developed by James Lovelock and Lynn Margulis herself, that the biosphere is in some sense a single organism, a self-regulating whole which operates by its own laws in such a way as to preserve life. In his new conclusion, Day refers to this notion in a way which makes clear that he supposes it to mean that we are safe whatever we do; because Gaia, our supernatural backer, will pay all the bills, and can be assumed to approve of our enterprises, since she has herself deliberately evolved us to make them. This is the direct opposite of the moral drawn by Lovelock and Margulis. Their point essentially was that our large-scale enterprises are trenching on a vast and delicate mechanism which we do not understand – that the survival of life itself has already been a far more chancy and fragile thing than is usually recognized, involving forces not yet understood by us, and the survival of any particular species, such as our own, must depend on a subtle balance among other life forms. The unlimited expansion of any particular one cannot fail to threaten this balance. If we personalize her, this Gaia does not look at all like Day's soft-hearted millionairess coming in at the end of the film to guarantee the hero's future. She is much more like Nemesis, or Charles Kingsley's Mrs Bedonebyasyoudid in *The Water Babies*. If she finds her system getting out of kilter because one element in it is insatiably greedy, she simply ditches that element as she has done so many others before. She is not in the least anthropocentric and has no special interest in intelligence. She is in fact impersonal, impartial Nature – not specially red in tooth and claw, but resolute to remain in general green and alive, and therefore liable to cross the projects of those who are acting so as to turn the green, thriving world into a desert. And if this resistance fails, she herself can no doubt be killed with all her children. No universal fail-safe mechanism protects either her or us.

Just what the Gaia Hypothesis means, and how it can best be related to biological science, is of course a large question. To see a non-reproducing entity as an organism, and a purposive one, without the benefit of past adaptation through selection, is not a straight-forward project. Still, supporters of the idea have brought forward detailed evidence to suggest that something of the kind may be needed, and the matter certainly deserves consideration. What concerns us in this book, however, is the function of the idea as a myth.

For this use it seems both sufficiently clear and very valuable. As an answer to anthropocentrism – as a reminder that we really are just one species among others, with no celestial warrant for general destruction – it can work and it can express much-needed truths. The startling enterprise of distorting it to do just the opposite – to boost anthropocentrism and increase over-confidence – is one more proof of the extraordinary force of existing pseudo-scientific superstitions.

8
Dazzling prospects

We want a man hag-ridden by the Future . . . dependent for his
faith on the success or failure of schemes whose end he will not
live to see. We want a whole race in pursuit of the rainbow's end,
never honest, nor kind, nor happy *now*, but always using as mere
fuel wherewith to heap the altar of the Future every real gift
which is offered them in the Present. . . . We have trained them
to think of the Future as a promised land which only heroes
attain – not as something which everyone reaches at the rate of
sixty minutes an hour, whatever he does, whoever he is.

C. S. Lewis, *The Screwtape Letters*, Chs XV and XXV

Claims for the future of science

Let us turn now to a slightly different kind of prophecy, concerned
mainly with the rosy future of science itself, but also indicating the
route by which it is to bring about a general reform of life. It is from
the sociobiologist Edward O. Wilson:

When mankind has achieved an ecological steady state, probably by the end of the twenty-first century, the internalization of
social evolution will be nearly complete. About this time biology
should be at its peak, with the social sciences maturing rapidly
. . . cognition will be translated into circuitry. Learning and
creativeness will be defined as the alteration of specific por-
tions of the cognitive machinery regulated by input from the
emotive centers. Having cannibalized psychology, the new
neurobiology will yield an enduring set of first principles for
sociology. . . . Skinner's dream of a culture predesigned for
happiness will surely have to wait for the new neurobiology.

A genetically accurate and hence completely fair code of ethics must also wait.[1]

This means, however, that we shall get it in the end, once the neurobiologists have done their stuff. Wilson admits indeed that some of us may not like this future world when we get it, partly, it seems, because of worries about genetic engineering. But this will be due to our unscientific attitude. It affects neither the dogmatic confidence of the prediction, nor the desirability of the outcome from the impersonal, scientific point of view.

The point about dogmatic confidence is interesting. Scrupulous moderation in making factual claims is commonly seen as a central part of the scientific attitude. Julian Huxley, listing the bad habits which infest religion, naturally mentions 'dogmatism' and 'aspiring to a false certitude' among them and explains that science corrects these vices.[2] Remarks like those just quoted do not on the face of it seem to meet this standard.

When I have complained of this sort of thing to scientists, I have sometimes met a surprising defence, namely, that these remarks appear in the opening or closing chapters of books, and that everybody knows that what is found there is not to be taken literally; it is just flannel for the general public. The idea seems to be that supplying such flannel constitutes a kind of a ritual. If so, it must surely strengthen our present unease, since addiction to ritual is another fault supposed to be the mark of religion. The point might of course just be the more practical one of selling books. But if grossly inflated claims to knowledge of the future are made for that reason, then there is either common dishonesty for personal profit, or an attempt to advance the cause of science by methods which disgrace it, and which (again) have always been considered a disgrace to religion. Putting these prophecies in a special part of the book does not disinfect them. It cannot be more excusable to peddle groundless predictions to the defenceless general public, who will take them to have the full authority of science, than to one's professional colleagues, who know much better what bees infest one's bonnet. These bold prophecies of an escalating future are often combined, as they are here, with the vision of one's own Science in a gold helmet finally crushing its academic rivals: again, scarcely a monument to scientific balance and caution.

Drawbacks of the escalator model

Is all this euphoria, however, actually dangerous? If the escalator myth really has got out of hand, what harm does it do?

In one way, certainly, it does much less harm than the egoistic myth of universal cut-throat competition. Optimism in general, even when it is muddled, tends to do less harm than pessimism. Faith in life, and in the human race, is certainly a better thing to have around than a supposedly science-based conviction of universal bloody-mindedness and hypocrisy. But once we are clear about that, we need to notice some objections, and as they have had much less attention than those which arise to the competitive myth, they may need more emphasis.

In the first place, faith in life and in the human race becomes much less evident when we turn from those who rely on continued natural growth, like Teilhard and Dobzhansky, to the champions of genetic engineering. Calling for surgical methods always shows less faith in the patient's constitution and more in the skills of the surgeon. The question, *in what do you put your faith?* is central to the whole enquiry. Those who put it in genetic engineering seem to give us what we now get so often here, an answer which misses the point of the question. They want us to put faith in certain techniques, or at most in the intellectual skills and capacities which make those techniques possible. But all these are means. What we need is to hear about aims, and about the faculties in all of us which reach out to those aims. What we get is a recommendation to entrust change to a certain set of experts, whose training has not called on them to pay any attention to conflicting aims at all.

The genetic engineering proposal, however, is not a necessary part of the escalator myth. Is there anything harmful about that myth itself, if we consider it in its more natural and consistent form as a simple prediction of steady, indefinite future human genetic progress to heights hitherto undreamed of?

I have already touched on the objection that this prediction, if it is taken as certain and infallible, gives a quite unwarranted sense of security, and can easily distract us from the need for other changes. If it is not taken as certain, but still as providing the only guideline towards safety, it admits the dangers but tells us, without argument, to rely on one particular way of escaping them rather than others, namely genetic engineering. And I think that those who do rely on it are in fact led by this way of thinking, not by any real evidence that this is a better prospect than other possible means of salvation. What, however, if no special question is raised about inevitability, but this progress is simply presented as the destiny offered to the human race? This somewhat vaguer picture is inspiring but a trifle dazzling. It may help us in assessing it to let the objector open the argument.

The central difficulty is that this story is arbitrarily human-centred, and that its view of humanity is at present arbitrarily intellect-centred. Its human-centredness distorts both evolutionary theory and our attitude to the natural world. By what right, and in what sense, can we consider ourselves as the directional pointer and aim-bearer of the whole evolutionary process? Does this mean what is often taken for granted today in controversy about the treatment of plants and animals, that all other organisms exist only as means to our ends? Kant and other philosophers have said this, many people believe it, yet it remains extremely obscure.[3] The idea that things are *there* for some external purpose seems to need a theological context, and this view did of course grow out of one. But that context will not subjugate everything to man. Certainly Judaeo-Christian thinking made the human race much more central than many other religions do, but it still considered man to be God's steward. Divine aims were always paramount, and God had created all his creatures for his own purposes, not for man's. Non-human beings count in this picture as having their own special value. Redwoods and pythons, frogs, moles and albatrosses are not failed humans or early try-outs for humans or tools put there to advance human development.

When this is spelled out, people today usually accept it, yet the escalator picture tends quietly and constantly to obscure it. Lamarck, who invented the escalator concept, did consider all non-human animals to be standing behind man, engaged on the same journey, and this still persisting idea does inevitably suggest that they are inferior and expendable. It obscures our enormous ignorance about their lives, about what it is like to be (say) a whale, a gorilla, an elephant, a mouse or a battery chicken, and supports our natural conviction that anything we don't do or experience can't have any value. The more we put aside this obviously hasty and inadequate myth, and notice the endless variety of existing creatures, the more we shall be driven to forget the linear metaphor of height, and return to the more Darwinian image of the radiating bush.

Which way is up?

Is there, however, still a fixed upward dimension? Does the bush have a human tip? Are we in some sense the point of the whole? I have never myself felt the need to say this, but very many people do, and the point must be taken seriously. It may well be that any intelligent species, able to meditate on such things, must in some way think of itself as central in the whole world, because in its own world it is so. It may be morally necessary to treat our own destiny as the most important thing conceivable, if only because we cannot easily conceive anything greater. But this by no means licenses us to separate it from all others and pursue it at their expense, nor does it mean, as escalator-fanciers sometimes kindly suggest, that our duty to those behind us is to help them to become like ourselves as quickly as possible. The moral consequences of a serious attitude to our own destiny are excellent, but those of a contemptuous attitude to other destinies are quite another matter. The two should not be linked at all.

Turning from morals to theory, could this way of thinking license us to predict that the next thing the bush will do is to grow taller? Change in human societies is now almost entirely a cultural, not a genetic matter, and it can as easily be for the worse as for the better. It is commonly recognized today that we badly need to be clear about this, since the belief in inevitable progress can be, and has been, used to justify bad changes which were preventable. Even, therefore, if we had reason to expect genetic change, this would not show that such change was good, nor that it was outside our control. And even if we had sound theoretical grounds for expecting the genetic development of our own species into something still greater and more distinctively human, this could scarcely show that we were the single supremely valuable object which gave point to the whole evolutionary process. There does not have to be any such one object. And since there are no such theoretical grounds either – since this expectation has no place in Darwinian theory, and came to Lamarck and Spencer simply as a welcome, self-justifying hunch – it is very remarkable that scientifically educated people still continue to ask the question which stands as title to the last chapter of William Day's book, from which I have already quoted, the question 'Where is evolution headed?'.[4]

The future as magnifying mirror

How does this question arise? If we look at the literature which asks it and attempts to give it answers, a very simple answer becomes almost unavoidable. It is a way of dramatizing morals. One can give a peculiar force to the praise and exaltation of particular ideals by presenting them as a piece of foresight, a glance at a real, attainable though perhaps distant future. This is an ancient, natural and legitimate device, which lies at the root of prophecy. Both bad and good futures can be used, but if the moral leverage is to work, both must be presented as only possible. There must still be time to work for this 'future' or avert it. Both author and reader must therefore be clear that the vision is an imaginary one, and this literature must be kept separate from the relatively humdrum business of prediction. Sober predictions about the likely future development of terrestrial life would not carry any such moral message. They would not necessarily make human affairs central at all, but would refer to them only in so far as they seem likely to affect the development of ecosystems. But the prophecies which now concern us are not in the least like this. They are quite simply exaltations of particular ideals within human life at their own epoch, projected on to the screen of a vague and vast 'future' – a term which, since Nietzsche and Wells, is not a name for what is particularly likely to happen, but for a fantasy realm devoted to the staging of visionary dramas.

In their content, these dramas plainly depend on the moral convictions of their author and of his age, not on scientific theories of any kind. Nietzsche, who laid down the ground-rules of this game, used Darwinian ideas and language as a pedestal for his own preferred ideal type, the unsocial, anarchic, creative individual, his enlarged and exalted self:

> Ye lonely ones of to-day; ye that stand apart, ye shall one day be a people; from you, that have chosen yourselves, a chosen people shall arise – and from it, the Superman. . . .
> And the Great Noon shall be when man standeth in the midst of his course between beast and Superman. . . . Dead are all gods; now will we that the Superman live.[5]

And, more prosaically:

> The problem I raise here is not what ought to succeed mankind (the human being is an *end*) but what type of human being one ought to *breed*, ought to *will*, as more valuable, more worthy of life, more certain of the future.[6]

The mark of this favoured and expected type is not just that he is free from the trammels of existing religion and morality, but that he is a fully unified human being, free from the many bad habits which at present divide our nature. He is to reunite spirit and intellect, which now wither in pretentious isolation, with their strong roots in the body, the imagination and the passions. Although externally he is isolated, contemptuous of social links with his fellows, internally he balances this isolation by the strongest possible integration of his nature. Indeed Nietzsche's hostility to outward social bonds is largely a protest against their tendency to fragment the individual's being. And, among contemporary influences which promote this fatal division, he thinks the exaltation of the bare intellect, especially in its scientific form, every bit as pernicious as the Christian religion:

> The harsh helot condition to which the tremendous extent of science has condemned every single person to-day is one of the main reasons why education and *educators* appropriate to fuller, richer, *deeper* natures are no longer forthcoming. Our culture suffers from nothing *more* than it suffers from the superabundance of presumptuous journeymen and fragments of humanity.[7]

And again:

> *From a doctorate exam.* – 'What is the task of all higher education?'
> – To turn a man into a machine – 'By what means?' He has to
> learn how to feel bored. 'How is this achieved?' – Through the
> concept of duty. . . . 'Who is the perfect man?' The civil
> servant.[8]

Thus Nietzsche; do we like his future? If not, the Jesuit biologist
Teilhard de Chardin offers us quite a different one, in which
Nietzsche's twin abominations, physical science and Christianity, are
both to be exalted and to find their final synthesis. It was Teilhard
who invented the phrase 'Omega man', using it to describe a future
being, raised above us both spiritually and intellectually, whose
destiny it is to complete the divine plan for this earth by perfecting it at
the mental level – to add a nöosphere, or intellectual realm, to the
living realm, or biosphere, which is already present. (Teilhard seems
also to have invented the term *biosphere*, and should be given the credit
for that useful move.) In this ideal future, the idea of brotherly love
and of the mystical union of individuals in the whole – an ideal which
would have been pure ratsbane to Nietzsche – plays a central part,
and traditional Christianity, however difficult it may be to fit in with
this ambitious scheme, is certainly still conceived as the main guiding
thread.

Scientists as Supermen

Do both these suggestions strike some readers today as a trifle crazy?
It cannot be too strongly emphasized how much this impression of
craziness depends on current moral and intellectual habits. What will
our own look like, to those who have ceased to share them? And what
is actually in the minds of those who make parallel suggestions today?

I shall go on using William Day's book *Genesis on Planet Earth*,
because it seems to me to put exceptionally clearly ideas which are
very widely accepted, and seldom as well expressed. Day writes
throughout as if only one sort of improvement could possibly be in
question, namely a rise in intelligence, and he treats *intelligence* as a
term which could not possibly be ambiguous or need analysis. To
increase this intelligence is, he says, the purpose of all life: an idea
which he presents as needing no defence or explanation. His language
about this is flagrantly teleological, indeed vitalist:

> Life has endured, generation after generation, producing more
> than can live, sacrificing many that the most fit may survive.
> Species have followed species, rung after rung, in a continuous
> climb of the ladder called evolution. And in that long ascent, life

has retained rapport with its surroundings by evolving its
window on the universe – intelligence.[9]

What is meant by speaking of intelligence as a window, and why
should such a window furnish the point of the whole? If windows
matter so much, must it not be because what we see through them is
important, and if it is, must there not be other valuable things besides
intelligence? Windows are a means. Is the function we are talking
about just the acquiring and ordering of information? or does it
include certain deep ways of responding to it? Those who originally
put this great stress on intelligence into European thought meant by it
something enormously wider than mere ordered storage. Both Plato
and Aristotle, who differed so much on countless other points, agreed
in making the point of the whole intellectual enterprise consist in the
contemplation to which it led: the awareness of a vast outer whole,
within which human thought operates, and of which it can form only
the faintest image. Day sees no such difficulty. Reality for him is what
we make it through science:

> It is into all reality that life, led by man, is expanding. Reality is
> no longer restricted to the horizons of the senses, but extends to
> the far reaches conceived by the mind. Physical reality may or
> may not be finite, for what exists is what we perceive, or identify
> as reality, and how far we can extend reality is uncertain.[10]

Resisting the temptation to go into all the implications of this – does
it actually mean that reality is what physicists say it is, and if so how
do they know what to say? – I stick to the point which now concerns
us, namely that the central business of the mind, the work for which
'life' has evolved it, is here physical science. Omega man emerges as
quite simply a superscientist. Only at one point does it look as if he
might have any other interests: where Day says that man's 'intelligence has evolved where, unlike any other form of life, he is touching
on a new dimension. It is man's spirituality, psyche and superego,
and that part of man [sic] that makes him the forerunner of Omega
man.'[11] But these mysterious dimensions have already been mentioned and been explained as being simply physical: 'real dimensions
of time and space, beyond our reach in size and perception'.[12]
Materialism is not being compromised. To settle that point finally,
Day goes on:

> A type of intelligence more evolved than man's could conceive
> of a reality *and exercise control over it* in a manner beyond our
> ability to comprehend. What comprehension *and powers over
> nature* Omega man will be able to command can only be
> suggested by man's image of the supernatural. (my italics)[13]

The mention of spirituality proves to have been only a ritual one. The real point of all this intelligence, and therefore of evolution itself, was, it turns out, simply to put more physical power in the hands of the quasi-deified human species, even though that species seems already to have a great deal more physical power than it knows what to do with.

9
Black holes:
Jacques Monod and the
isolation of 'science'

Let, unaccompanied, that psalm begin
Which deals most harshly with the fruits of Sin.

John Betjeman

Darker forecasts

A similar exclusive exaltation of science appears, with some interesting differences, at the end of Steven Weinberg's excellent and informative little book *The First Three Minutes: A Modern View of the Origin of the Universe*. His last chapter is called 'Epilogue: the prospect ahead', and it ends thus:

> The more the universe seems comprehensible, the more it also seems pointless.
>
> But if there is no solace in the fruits of our research, there is at least some consolation in the research itself. Men and women are not content to comfort themselves with tales of gods and giants, or to confine their thoughts to the daily affairs of life; they also build telescopes and satellites and accelerators, and sit at their desks for endless hours working out the meaning of the data they gather. The effort to understand the universe is one of the very few things that lifts human life a little above the level of farce, and gives it some of the grace of tragedy.[1]

Since virtually the whole book has been devoted to expounding astrophysics, not to discussing it as an occupation, and certainly not to discussing other occupations with which it might compete, Weinberg's readers might find this an unexpected blow. They might feel rather shaken and degraded by the sudden revelation that their lives are probably valueless, and they might also ask the reasonable question: how does Weinberg know? And what has he in mind about the rest of the few competing non-farcical elements in life? Is there any hope for cultures other than our own, which do not build telescopes and satellites and accelerators, that is for most of the people there have ever been, of doing anything worth while at all?

What Weinberg means about tragedy has emerged in the previous paragraph. It turns out, he says, that this is an 'overwhelmingly hostile universe', hostile in the sense that it existed long before us and is not going to preserve us for ever. On current predictions, it will all eventually vanish, and when the conditions which we inhabit go, they will take us with them. Why this should make us denounce the universe as hostile rather than – if we are going to be anthropomorphic – make us call it generous for producing and sustaining us, Weinberg does not say. The script which he follows here seems to be the quite widely accepted one produced by Jacques Monod, who, as we have seen,[2] states as the message of science the claim that man 'must realise that, like a gypsy, he lives on the boundary of an alien world'. This is surprising news for evolutionary biologists, whose science has for the last century been busy delivering exactly the opposite message, namely that man was born here and had better acknowledge the place as his native home. What is going on?

Monod's picture is of great interest. Its wide success shows how strongly scientists, and others who put their faith in science, have felt the need for a clearer articulation of that faith. Popper's determined narrowing of science could not of itself provide that articulation, because it was too negative. It simply declared by fiat that only certain things could be allowed to count as science, and surrounded them on the map by an area marked *terra incognita*. For this area the word 'metaphysics' was indeed used. But it did not carry there its proper meaning as the study of certain central topics in philosophy. Whatever Popper meant by it, to most of its hearers it was just a general abusive term for non-scientific thinking, often read as simply synonymous with 'nonsense'. Thus the theory of evolution itself was for some time excluded from science as metaphysical, though it is manifestly a historical theory, and this was widely seen as downgrading its importance. (The idea that a theory could have both historical *and* scientific aspects seems not to have crossed anyone's mind.) Geography and geology, too, because of the particularity of their subject-matter, were viewed as parts of metaphysics rather than as separate sciences, and cosmology naturally came under similar suspicion.

In short, just at the time when the special, unique value of science, and its distinctness from all other studies, were being most strongly asserted, its frontiers were cast into grave confusion. Moreover, the very reasons for valuing it so highly became hard to state. Discussing them would have involved discussing also the values of other ideals to which it is related, and this was ruled to fall outside scientific business. The best way out would probably have been to revise the map which isolated science, noting its connections with other studies, and making any exclusions which were needed much clearer and more selective. Marxist and Freudian thinking needed to be more closely examined, their merits conceded and their defects more sharply defined. And the meaning of 'science' itself, with the implied compliment it conveyed, needed to be made much clearer.

Monod, however, offered a most welcome and seductive dramatization of the existing confused position instead of this rather gruelling programme. He simply took the Popperian map and projected existentialist colouring on to it to satisfy the imagination. For *terra incognita* he invited us to read 'tragic darkness'. For the accidental, temporary isolation of science from other studies, we should read 'the incurable isolation of man'. We should accept the mortification of our reason produced by the impossibility of extending our understanding beyond the borders of science as a test of our courage; authenticity would demand that we made no attempt to breach it. In his anxiety to get rid of irrelevant thinking, Monod made huge inroads on the province of thought. This move was only made to look plausible by the importation of a whole new mass of feeling, of a drama which did duty for argument. It is no accident which leads Weinberg to talk of farce and tragedy. Monod's thinking, like Sartre's, is essentially melodramatic.

The attack on 'animism'

Monod's aim is to get rid of what he calls animism, a term which he uses very widely. It covers, not just the idea that a conscious, purposive being has devised the universe to produce us, but also any notion of laws which have made our presence here necessary. 'We would like', he says, 'to think ourselves necessary, inevitable, ordained from all eternity. All religions, nearly all philosophies, and even a part of science testify to the unwearying, heroic effort of mankind desperately denying its own contingency.'[3] He notes with alarm the strength of this tendency:

> At the very core of certain ideologies claiming to be founded on science, the animist projection, in a more or less disguised form, turns up again. . . . It was not Teilhard who discovered the idea

of re-establishing the old animist covenant with nature, or of founding a new one through a universal theory according to which the evolution of the biosphere culminating in man would be part of the smooth onward flow of cosmic evolution itself. This idea was in fact the central theme of nineteenth-century scientistic progressism. One finds it at the very heart of Spencer's positivism and of Marx and Engels' dialectical materialism.[4]

Monod was surely right to resist this over-ambitious reliance on the escalator model and the inflated creeds which express it. They are the source of the superstitions we have been examining, and of much other evil too. The difficulty is to cut out what is noxious in them without slicing into either the living tissue of science itself or other necessary parts of our thought. Monod ran together under the name of animism at least four quite distinct ideas: (1) that the human race is a necessary phenomenon, predictable according to scientific laws; (2) that it provides the central purpose of the universe; (3) that evolution is an escalator leading smoothly up to it; and (4) that it is continuous with, and at home in, the surrounding world.

The first three are indeed mistakes, but different mistakes; the fourth is an important truth. Against all four equally, Monod sets the one idea of our 'contingency', which accordingly gets very obscure. Much of his book consists of scientific arguments directed against the first of the four ideas. He brings evidence to show that chance has intruded at various stages in the development of life, notably in producing mutations and in whatever mysterious and highly improbable process set life itself going in the first place. He wants to show sharp discontinuity, first between the inanimate world and life, which will thus become a surd, unpredictable, alien event within it, and then between the entire physical world and our minds. Monod's aim is to introduce enough disorder into the cosmos to quash the argument from design altogether. He thinks that earlier mechanistic materialism failed to do this because, in presenting the universe as a perfect superclock, it left too much temptation to bring back the clockmaker. Laplace, the eighteenth-century theorist who first supplied science with the alluring model of the physical world as a faultless clock with no maker, had ruled that God must never be re-introduced, but (says Monod) he is not being obeyed. Modern science must complete his work by showing that there is real confusion in the cosmic order. This will finally discredit animism – though Monod admits that atheistic discipline will still be very hard to maintain.

Order without an orderer

It is a very interesting question how far it is possible to separate the sense of order in this way from any notion of an ordering mind. This is a much bigger project than that of merely casting doubts on any particular creed or faith through which that sense has been expressed. Certainly, the more anthropomorphic a creed is, the more the notion of an arbitrary, personal will enters into thoughts of creation. And clearly that notion is hostile to science. But the objection to an arbitrary will is that it runs counter to what mind demands, that is, counter to order. And order is what science studies; if it is to proceed on any given subject-matter, it has to assume in advance that there will be order there, that it will be penetrable to mind. It seems quite possible that from the human point of view at least the notions of mind and order are at root inseparable, that order is almost inevitably perceived as the expression of mind. T. H. Huxley, that stern and splendid old fighter against all that was base in religion, has some very interesting remarks about this:

> If imagination is used within the limits laid down by science, disorder is unimaginable. If a being endowed with perfect intellectual and aesthetic faculties, but devoid of the capacity for suffering pain, either physical or moral, were to devote his utmost powers to the investigation of nature, the universe would seem to him to be a sort of kaleidoscope, in which, at every successive moment of time, a new arrangement of parts of exquisite beauty and symmetry would present itself, and each of them would show itself to be the logical consequence of the preceding arrangement, under the conditions which we call the laws of nature. Such a spectator might well be filled with that *Amor intellectualis Dei*, the beatific vision of the *vita contemplativa*, which some of the greatest thinkers of all ages, Aristotle, Aquinas, Spinoza, have regarded as the only conceivable eternal felicity; and the vision of illimitable sufferings, as if sensitive beings were unregarded animalcules which had got between the bits of glass of the kaleidoscope, which mars the prospect to us poor mortals, in no wise alters the fact that *order is lord of all, and disorder only a name for that part of the order which gives us pain.*[5]

Do Monod's modern discoveries really affect this position? It is hard to see how they could. Huxley is not relying on any simple, Laplacian idea of a clock, a single universal mechanism. He is talking more widely about any order which satisfies the intellect. The only scientific area, among those which Monod cites, that breaks with the normal idea of causal order is quantum mechanics. This does not posit chaos instead; it substitutes a statistical order. And physicists, in so far as they are satisfied with this concept, accept it as penetrable to mind. They are not in fact wholly satisfied with it, because of difficulties in relating it to some of their other concepts. They are therefore currently busy in revising their epistemology. They seem likely to move further away from regarding this or any other of their models as final and direct descriptions of the world, and towards treating each as having only limited and provisional use. It would accordingly be very naïve to use quantum mechanics as Monod apparently wants to, to prove a lapse of order as an objective fact.

Chance as pointlessness

That case apart, the phenomena he cites as 'chance' do not involve breaks in casual sequence, but only happenings which he calls '"absolute coincidences"; those which result from the intersection of two totally independent chains of events.'[6] He gives the example of a doctor killed by the accidental fall of a workman's hammer. This is a surprising idea, because it is not clear that, objectively speaking, there are any absolute coincidences at all. In the causal network, no two chains are independent, and the identification of chains itself requires an interest. Besides, we would still call this event a chance one even if doctor and workman were closely connected causally, for instance if they were twin brothers working on the same job. The use of chance here is surely the everyday one where it means 'something irrelevant to purpose'. And this is actually the only sense it can bear in Monod's references to genetics also.

His point is that neither the mechanism of mutation nor the changing environment is subject to any purpose of the developing organisms whose evolution they control. This is no doubt a fair point against his second target, the belief that the universe was made for man. It is true that neither in our own development nor in that of the organisms we must deal with does there seem to have been a special directional control for our interests. Natural selection is no more, if no less, on our side than on that of the wasp or the tapeworm. We have been lucky so far, but that need not last. This target, however, is an easy one to hit and certainly does not require the special scientific reasonings which Monod employs. There are plenty of other objections to it besides the scientific oddity of the notion of the human race as necessary.

Chance as unpredictability

The notion that mankind might be necessary in the sense of being strictly predictable, like the falling of a dropped stone, seems to be something of a straw man. Biology does not deal in that sort of predictability for large-scale events. Because living systems are so complex, it needs constantly to vary its concepts according to its subject-matter, and is not given to claiming necessity for historical occurrences, though it often has a good deal to say about probability. The crude alternatives of pure chance and pure necessity which Monod deals in are not suited to it at all. As Dobzhansky remarks:

> This dichotomy, applied by Monod to biological as well as human evolution, is spurious. Evolution is neither necessary, in the sense of being predestined, nor is it a matter of chance or accident. It is governed by natural selection, in which ingredients of chance and antichance are blended in a way which makes the dichotomy meaningless, and which renders evolution to be a creative process. . . . The chance in mutation is blind, but it is neither 'pure' nor 'absolutely free'. . . . Natural selection is an antichance agent. Its action however does not amount to necessity. Its outcome is unpredictable in the long run.[7]

In short, Monod's picture, in which certain limited areas of pure necessity – isolated clocks – stand isolated in a howling desert of entirely unpredictable chaos, is a travesty. No doubt he was encouraged to develop it by the 'beanbag' genetic theories already mentioned, which made the behaviour of genes themselves look much more confused and chancy than it is now known to be. It was even being suggested that genes were directly affected by perturbations at the quantum-mechanical level. As it happens, the whole movement of genetics in the last half-century has been towards a much more orderly picture of gene behaviour.[8] Genes are now increasingly seen both as simpler in their internal structure and as much more closely connected together than used to be thought. Working usually in large, fairly stable blocks, they have nothing like the wild range of possible variation which Monod supposed. His views seem to have been considerably out of date in his own day, and the scientific ideas which led him on to envisage the genetic process as a 'gigantic lottery' are no longer plausible.

Venerating the cosmos: the pantheist vision

That need not make much difference, of course, to Monod's central attack on 'animism', which is not really concerned with the role of necessity in biology, but with the dramatization of evolution. What Huxley said is still true. The main difficulties here are not theoretical; they are moral. The real objection to accepting and revering the universe as an ordered whole does not spring from the presence of disorder in it. Indeed it is hard to see what could give us theoretical ground for positing any such disorder; quantum mechanics surely does not do so. It springs from the apparently disorderly distribution of such things as pleasure and pain – from the difficulty of seeing how this pattern can fit into an acceptable underlying purpose.

Is it right to have faith, as the great religions do, in the existence of such a purpose? Does our acceptance of theoretical order reasonably lead us on, as Spinoza thought and Huxley did not, to recognize a level at which it merges into the intellectual love of God? (The world had not, of course, grown grimmer between Spinoza's day and Huxley's; Spinoza wrote in a Europe ravaged by the Thirty Years War and was no sort of sentimental optimist. The level must be deep indeed.) This question cannot be settled, as Comte suggested and as Freud believed,[9] by a ruling about the human life cycle, declaring all favourable answers to it to be *ipso facto* childish. Our current local notion of adulthood is a peculiar one, directly produced by positivistic thinking; it cannot serve as an independent ground for it. Nor can the question be settled simply by the principle of parsimony. That principle rapidly begins to flounder when it gets away from simple cases. False economy is very common among people who rely too readily on it. As we are seeing, extravagance is not eliminated merely by becoming anti-religious, and thoughts which are designed to be sternly reductive often compensate by strange, illicit expansions elsewhere. In fact when we encounter a specially harsh reduction, officially launched in the name of parsimony, our first question should probably be 'and what are these savings being used to pay for?'

10

Freedom and the Monte Carlo drama _____

The bastard! He doesn't exist.

J.-P. Sartre on God

Moral scepticism and its exceptions

With this large question of whether all viewing of the universe as
directional, all Spinozan reverence for it, is mistaken, Monod, however, cannot help us. Long before this issue arises, his discussion has
settled the matter with a blanket rejection, not just of the idea of
purpose in nature, but of all significant connection between ourselves
and the universe around us. Monod's 'postulate of objectivity', which
excludes cosmic purposes, also implies for him that we are strangers
here in the sense of inhabiting a meaningless world, which has no
value in it and can give us absolutely no guidance about values. As has
been pointed out before over Sartre's doctrines, the notion of our 'self'
which this implies – the abstract, non-terrestrial will – is a very
strange one, apparently a descendant, still latent in French thought,
of the isolated Cartesian pure soul. This entity becomes necessary
because Monod, following Sartre, apparently recognizes only two
possible sources of morality: either the direct command of God or the
pure fiat of this free human will. Having displaced God in favour of
chance, he again follows Sartre in carefully excluding all our natural
sources of motivation and the background of cultural patterns built
from them. This makes it easy to rule that the world is meaningless
and all value-judgment arbitrary. Meaning is connection, so it can
always be removed from a pattern by cutting it up into sufficiently
small pieces. And with black-and-white photography, the world can
easily be made to look colourless.

This is a perverse move. Moral thinking is not something like an electric light, which can be switched off at a distance in this way by removing the idea of God as a kind of power-station. It is a branch of social thinking, articulating standards which necessarily arise in dealing with the chronic conflicts endemic to human life. It has a hundred sources, not just one, and seems to be a necessary feature of the interaction between intelligent beings. (Darwin may well have been right that any sufficiently intelligent social being would need to develop it.[1]) Accordingly, a great deal of its substance arises from the conditions of human life and is not arbitrary at all. Where it is arbitrary, we view it as changeable and we frequently do change it. But to do so we refer to deeper, more general underlying considerations which by no means depend on our wills. Everybody, however theoretically sceptical about morals, recognizes some such considerations, and argument designed – as Monod's certainly is – to change people's conduct could not possibly be carried on without presupposing them.

This becomes luminously clear when Monod, like Sartre, wants to deliver a value-judgment of his own, immune to general scepticism. For Sartre, the exception was a rather general one about the value of 'authenticity' itself, which is the courage to admit one's freedom. It is indeed scarcely possible to argue the need for this without tacitly admitting both the general possibility of moral argument and the particular importance of the standards which one appeals to in doing it. But this means that other positions can also be put. To establish authenticity as the only virtue needs a lot of argument. The complicated epicycles of existentialist theory are there to do this job; they are not very successful. Monod, however, has a much bigger and more awkward article to smuggle through his own customs, something far too gross to get past any set of inspectors not already dedicated to importing it. He wants to give a special status to science, to show it as the one thing which does have real, undeniable value. Since he has just stressed that no values are given and that we must be equally free to accept or reject anything, this is hard. Monod fights back stoutly. There is, he says, only one ideal which can be freely chosen, and that is knowledge:

> In the ethic of knowledge, *it is the ethical choice of a primary value that is the foundation.* The ethic of knowledge thereby differs radically from animist ethics, which all claim to be based on the 'knowledge' of immanent religious or 'natural' laws which are supposed to impose themselves on man. The ethic of knowledge does not impose itself on man; *on the contrary, it is he who imposes it on himself,* making it the *axiomatic* condition of authenticity for all discourse and all action.[2]

Other ideals, he implies, can only be chosen thoughtlessly, without freedom. And it is 'animistic' to choose with reference to any purpose which is treated as already given, since the universe itself is purposeless. Neither side of this contention can possibly work. On the one hand, other ideals certainly can be freely and deliberately chosen. Sartre's choice of freedom itself is only one obvious example. Moral philosophy is full of careful arguments supporting such choices. Many of the arguers object radically to the simple plan which Monod adopts of picking one single, all-sufficient 'primary value' and treating everything else merely as a means to it. Others use that plan, but argue for a different value. Anyone who wanted to make knowledge the despot here would have to face the moral arguments for at least the most obvious rival contenders such as happiness, freedom, pleasure and aesthetic experience. Failure to face them certainly does not establish the champions of knowledge as specially free, but rather as lazy-minded and dogmatic. As for the special claims of knowledge itself, it seems odd to suggest that our pursuit of it involves no given purpose and no natural taste. We want it because we are naturally inquisitive. That is a contingent fact about us which might well have been otherwise. And the special objects which we enquire about, including those which the sciences study at any given time, are also contingent. They depend on social and personal factors of the most varied kinds. They are not arbitrary. Our natural interest and enjoyment of these studies is a good reason for us to pursue them individually, and the value which our society as a whole puts on the results is a good reason for it to make them possible. But there are also other occupations for which we have good reasons. The priority systems by which we place them all in our lives cannot be settled from one side only. A really free, deliberate judgment would need to look at all of them. Obsessive, partisan judgment is very far from free.

Monod's determination to avoid all such confrontation, and to hand down his value system as unquestionable, is very striking. He points out that his 'postulate of objectivity' is impossible to demonstrate, but he says nevertheless that it is 'consubstantial with science, and has guided the whole of its prodigious development for three centuries' and calls for 'censorship' to preserve its purity.[3] Accordingly, he presents 'objective knowledge as the *only* source of real truth'.[4] So what sort of truth do we deal with in everyday life, in personal relations or in the study of history? And since scientists frequently disagree and change their theories, which scientific truth are we to accept? We would surely need some further explanation before we could make any sense of this claim. David Bohm reasonably remarks on the extreme dogmatism, shared by Monod and by the religious authorities, especially in earlier times, when religion played a dominant role in human affairs. One could indeed regard the postulate of objectivity as a paraphrase of former articles of religious faith which people were required to accept. . . . To carry the parallel further, it was supposed by the church that, if man is to be good, he must 'freely' assent to God's will (as interpreted by the religious authorities). . . . Both the religious authorities and Monod agree on the need for a strict 'censorship' of views contrary to what is right and good. They both talk in terms of 'commandments'. In effect, Monod is proposing that objective scientific knowledge should replace religion, not only as a source of knowledge of the world, but also as a source of authority which determines the whole of man's being, even his innermost feelings and aspirations.[5]

Understanding the primacy of knowledge

If, then, we decide to set this dogmatism aside and question the special status of science, do we find any special virtues attending the ideal of knowledge and giving it a special status? There are in fact several, which exalters of the intellect from Plato on have celebrated. They have shown, for instance, that knowledge of some kind or other is needed in the pursuit of most other human ideals. Without it, the virtues tend to be blind and activities tend to be misdirected. But this is not a defence that Monod can use. Knowledge for him does not mean these various kinds of insight; it means physical science. Moreover, he, like Sartre, wants to write off all these other ideals as optional and dispensable, so that contributing to them cannot be important. Alternatively, Plato and Aristotle gave knowledge a special status by arguing that it was in the nature of the soul to reach out through contemplation to something greater than itself; knowledge simply was that contemplation. But Monod does not believe that there is any such greater thing, nor that the soul has a nature. And again, this still would not give the palm to the right kind of knowledge. What he needs is an argument for the pre-eminence of physical science, not as part of a cluster of ideals, but as *the* one to which all the rest should be subordinated. He carefully explains this, in case any of us still feel nostalgic for the others: 'As for the highest human qualities, courage, altruism, generosity, creative ambition, the ethic of knowledge both recognizes their sociobiological origin and affirms their transcendent value *in the service of the ideal it defines.*' (my italics)[6]

No suitable argument supports this priority, and though Monod is probably unaware of it, the claim is as arbitrary as any in the long history of moral fraudulence. Dressed up in this way to look like metaphysical and scientific reasoning, it becomes very pernicious. What sort of a world would that be, in which all the aims of science were attained, and no other aims were even considered to have the slightest independent importance?

The drama of parental callousness

Weinberg, for his part, quite possibly does not mean seriously to endorse Monod's crude subordination of all other human ideals to that of scientific knowledge. In general he is a scrupulous writer, very careful to control most of the dramas lurking in his subject. When he puts physics among 'the very few' non-farcical human activities, he may not mean to narrow the range of these much further than the rest of us would. But the language is strong, and taken together with his remarks just before it does suggest melodrama. Two things, I think, are going wrong.

First, there is the tone of personal aggrievement and disillusion, which seems to depend, both in him and Monod, on failure to get rid of the animism or personification which they officially denounce. An inanimate universe cannot be hostile. To call it that is to reproach it for not being the divine parent of earlier belief. Only in a real, conscious human parent could uncaringness equal hostility. Weinberg's mention of farce seems meant to imply the malicious callousness of such a parent, perhaps of one who leads a child on to expect affection and then rejects it. Monod seems to express the same unreasonable disappointment when he says that man lives 'on the boundary of an alien world, a world that is deaf to his music and as indifferent to his hopes as it is to his sufferings or his crimes'.[7] Certainly if we expect the non-human world around us to respond to us as a friendly human would, we shall be disappointed. But this does not put it in the position of a callously indifferent human. What we can rightly demand and get from the natural world around us is not this kind of social attention but something quite different – a setting of living things and creatures to which we are attuned, and to whose music we for our part are far from deaf. Because we can get this, and do get it unless we treat the natural world too brutally, we are simply not in the position of the lonely, alien intruders pictured by Sartre and Monod. And because the natural world is not a person, neither is it an enemy whom we can heroically resist. The drama of Ajax defying the lightning falls flat once we have demystified electric charges as modern physics tells us to.

The second trouble concerns time and chance. For Weinberg, in the sad reflections noticed on p. 75, what reduces most of human life to farce is not just the element of indeterminacy in particle physics but also the shortness of our time-span. As he says there:

> It is almost irresistible for humans to believe that we have some special relation to the universe, that human life is not just a more-or-less farcical outcome of a chain of accidents reaching back to the first three minutes, but that we were somehow built in from the beginning. . . . It is very hard to realise that this all is just a tiny part of an overwhelmingly hostile universe. It is even harder to realise that this present universe has evolved from an unspeakably unfamiliar early condition, and faces a future extinction of endless cold or intolerable heat. The more the universe seems comprehensible, the more it also seems pointless.[8]

The casino fantasy

What is there here that is genuinely alarming, and what is added drama? First, in what way does the 'chain of accidents' reduce human life to a 'more or less farcical outcome'? Talk of accidents seems again to anthropomorphize and personalize. The word 'accident' is value-laden; it implies that someone slipped up. It suggests human careless-ness intruding to spoil an ambitious design. Monod makes a revealing comment:

> Immanence is alien to modern science. Destiny is written as and while, not before, it happens. . . . The universe was not preg-nant with life nor the biosphere with man. Our number came up in the Monte Carlo game. Is it surprising that, like the person who has just made a million at the casino, we should feel strange and a little unreal?[9]

This again is melodrama. A casino is a human institution, devised to serve specific human motives. 'Chance' in a casino context means the deliberate randomizing of a small section of human affairs as a special way of redistributing income. Gambling language is indeed often used for probability calculations because gamblers have been so interested in them, and it can be quite harmless there. But this does not license Monod to import the special motivations which produce gambling, and conclude that the universe is really just a vast casino. The idea of gambling cannot be used to convey meaninglessness. It is an idea packed with meaning. The casino image is every bit as anthropomorphic as the familiar argument from design. God re-appears as a sinister croupier, a president of the immortals deliberately refusing to organize things because it amuses him more to let the wheel spin and generate farces. Biology, too, is strangely distorted here. The biosphere certainly was pregnant with us, among its other children, and the universe with life. It is quite anti-scientific to suppose that, in the development of life, sudden vast leaps like winning a million could take place. 'Immanence' is of course a vague term, but some degree of suitability between effects and causes is a necessary presupposition of all organized thinking, not only of the sciences. 'Chance' in the sense in which it can be credited with contributing to either life or the human race simply means 'relatively remote causes'. Ignorance of causes is the only proper sense for the term to bear in biology, and in most other scientific contexts. In particle physics it may indeed now have the stronger meaning of actual indeterminacy. But in no science can it mean that slightly sinister and underhand deity worshipped by gamblers, Fortune on her wheel, whose presence is needed if we are to grow dramatic and talk of farce. And it cannot show us as strangers, in the way in which the gambler is a stranger to his fortune.

Two things make the situation of the Monte Carlo winner 'strange and unreal'. His million is unearned, and it comes to him in one enormous, sudden dollop. (Even an earned million could be disturbing if it appeared unexpectedly all at once like this.) Neither of these things is true of human life. The original human evolutionary niche was gradually earned in exactly the same way as other evolutionary niches – by ages of slow, patient adaptation, which fitted our ancestors to occupy it and ensured that it had plenty of meaning for them. (Our later raids on the evolutionary niches of others are of course a different matter, but then that is not what Monod is talking about.) Of course human beings did not earn their niche in the wild sense of entirely inventing it by their own power. No organism needs or expects to do that. The environment came to them from outside as a set of uncovenanted blessings and difficulties; raw material to deal with. Their contribution was to adapt, both genetically and culturally, so as to deal with their circumstances. Their given material, moreover, included the natural limitations on their powers of adapting. The element of chance in genetic mutation is simply a part of this background of given capacities and incapacities. For human beings living their lives, everything in their natural constitution comes from outside anyway as luck, in the sense that they did not make it, any more than they made the physical conditions outside them. This kind of luck does not compromise their independence, because the notion of independence makes no sense except in a world already containing given problems which one is to show independence in solving. The idea of a creature totally self-dependent is an empty one. Freedom can only be exercised against a wide background of constraints. As for luck or chance in the further, quite different sense in which scientists, when they come to study the matter, may find it if they conclude that a process is random and unpredictable for purposes of theory, that is an internal matter for science, without bearing on the meaning of life. Accordingly, neither the 'genetic lottery' nor quantum mechanics has any special significance for the way in which we should regard our lives. We have no need at all to follow Monod's peculiar path of dramatizing both these, first by concentrating on them to the exclusion of the much more numerous non-random areas of science, which contribute a great deal to making our lives intelligible, and then by describing his chosen areas in the language of the casino. That language invokes a third, much narrower notion of dependence on 'luck' in which it means the deliberate parasitism of people who choose to live by gambling rather than by earning their keep. Since this is the only sense of luck in which any alternative exists to living by luck and accepting it, it is the only sense which involves anything discreditable or degrading, and so the only one which will give any sense to the notion of 'farce'.

11

Scientific education and human transience

> The candle that is set up in us shines bright enough for all our purposes.
>
> John Locke

Living with a crippled intellect

It is not surprising, however, that Monod's story has had so much success, especially among scientists. In its lively, existentially coloured package, it offers a way of combining the general scepticism and acceptance of confusion about moral questions which is widely professed today with a firm, saving exception for confidence in the value of science. This fits the world-picture acquired by very many people in the course of a scientific education, an education which trains them in scientific thinking, and greatly exaggerates the precision possible to it, while doing very little to teach them the ways of thinking which they will need for other purposes – personal, political, psychological, historical, metaphysical and all the rest. Since these purposes are central to life and call for a great deal of thought, especially in changing times, those whose intellect has been cramped by this kind of foot-binding process into a specialized use experience a very painful sense of confusion when other issues come before them. The discrepancy between their confident use of highly trained intelligence in their work and their helplessness on other issues threatens to tear them apart and attacks the roots of their self-respect. (Scholars in general are of course to some extent subject to this trouble, but the physical sciences tend to have a method and a subject-matter even more remote from everyday problems than the rest.) In this emergency, Monod appears with the balm of a metaphysical proof that their plight is inescapable. He declares that science is indeed the only field where thought is possible. Everything else must be left to choice: not reasonable choice, but choice in the Existentialist sense of a blind, inarticulate act of will. For those who may still hesitate, he stands ready with a bracing draught of dogmatic puritan morality to enforce this mortification of the intellect:

> Cold and austere, proposing no explanation but imposing an ascetic renunciation of all other spiritual fare, this idea could not allay anxiety; it aggravated it instead. It claimed to sweep away at a stroke the tradition of a hundred thousand years. . . . With nothing to recommend it but a certain puritan arrogance, how could such an idea be accepted? It was not; it still is not.[1]

Nevertheless, he insists, it ought to be; heroes should take their cold bath without flinching. Only bad habits and the weakness of our flesh stand in the way. Flattered and impressed, his public is naturally inclined to think that its duty has now become clear. The pangs felt by an intellect bound down and distorted from its full natural use must be borne and disregarded as merely accidents of our mortal condition. Thought must be abstained from except in the only place where it can be performed with perfect success and purity: the laboratory. To carry them through this ordeal, scientists will always have that strong though not very nutritious stimulant, spiritual pride, grounded on the conviction of being the only human group that has any worthwhile occupation at all.

It is interesting to contrast this embittered, querulous form of Stoicism with the quieter, less pretentious Roman variety that is its ancestor. Marcus Aurelius, for instance, thought it fairly important to be contented:

> Whether the world subsists by a fortuitous concourse of atoms, or an intelligent Nature presides over it, let this be laid down as a maxim, that I am a part of a whole, governed by its own nature. . . . I shall never be displeased with whatever is allotted me by that whole. . . . Let us then employ properly this moment of time allotted to us by fate, and leave the world contentedly, like a ripe olive dropping from its stalk, speaking well of the soil that produced it, and of the tree that bore it.[2]

This does not seem to be any more 'animistic' than Weinberg's notion of a hostile universe, and it is certainly better biology than Monod's suggestion of an alien universe to which we do not really belong at all.

A matter of scale

By now, however, it should be clear how these unquestionably depressing thoughts have come to replace the euphoria generated by the escalator model. It is all a matter of perspective. To the astrophysicist who stands right back from the biological picture, any escalation of life, however prolonged, is a mere hiccup. All forecasts for humanity, even when they include extensions through genetic engineering and space travel, come to the same thing in the end. H. G. Wells understood this clearly and stressed it in *The Time Machine* and elsewhere. But in the excitement of twentieth-century technology it seems somehow to have been largely forgotten, and recent escalator fantasies have been developed with little regard to it. Once remembered, however, it is liable to puncture them completely. It does so because they depend so heavily on the pay-off pattern, the notion that the value of anything lies in its consequences. Jam is always tomorrow, never today. If, then, we decide that jam will one day cease, the hope of all intervening days is at once destroyed and jam as such is proved never to have been anything but a cruel illusion. Moreover science itself, which was regarded as the main source of faith in future jam, now deals the death-blow to all such hopes through a ruling in astrophysics. Had the doctrine of continuous creation prevailed over that of the big bang, things might, in some people's view, have been different; there would still be hope for us. Others, however, will point out with Weinberg that it would still be true that the universe existed for a very long time before us. They will also perhaps wonder whether descendants immeasurably distant from us in time would be much comfort. Whichever way you look at it, on a cosmic scale we are very small.

Living with eternity

What, however, forces us to use either the cosmic scale or the exclusive pay-off pattern when we are looking for meaning? It may be true that, as Weinberg says, 'it is almost irresistible for humans to believe that we have some special relation to the universe.'[3] But ideas about what that relation is vary greatly, and scarcely any can have been so ambitiously complacent as those developed in the west in the last century. Many cultures before us have expected an end to the universe. The Norse expected that end in Ragnarok, and thought of the special relation of humans to it as simply a duty laid on them to help in that final battle, doing what they could to stave off the ruin which would still finally engulf not only them, but everything else that was good. Others indeed have expected, like the Stoics, that the

destruction of the world would be followed by a new age and a new
cycle. Indeed, astrophysics itself seems now to envisage this as one
possibility, involving an indefinite sequence of big bangs. But it is not
at all clear what sort of identification this idea licenses with the age
that is to follow. It certainly cannot work through the survival of the
human species, or the continuation of any single activity known to us.
Many cultures too, such as the Hindus and the ancient Greeks, have
seen the procession of the ages not as static but as steadily deteriorat-
ing. And to many, such as the Buddhists, hope does not lie in any
reversal of this process, but within, in becoming free, through fuller
understanding, from the wheel of being itself.

These very varied beliefs, and others equally far from our own, have
not prevented people from finding meaning in their lives. Indeed,
many have insisted that a full acceptance of the dark perspectives
around us is absolutely necessary if one is even to start on an effective
search for that meaning. The problem of evil is not an accidental
difficulty for religion; it is the starting-point from which the search
that sometimes leads to religion begins. This realization of evil starts,
of course, not at the cosmic end but from individual death and
disaster. And the forecasts just mentioned are not really meant as
scientific predictions, but as symbolic descriptions of how the world
works and what we ought to expect from it. Weinberg, however, is
surely making just that same use of his own forecast in the passage
quoted. The fact that his forecast is actually a scientific one does not
prevent this. But it does tend to confuse us about the kind of authority
which his words carry. For those of us who know nothing about
astrophysics, Weinberg and his sources are authorities about that.
There we ought to believe them. But this does not give them any
authority at all on the choice of suitable symbols for human destiny.
Here their stories must stand on their own merits as myths. No special
standing attaches either to the casino story or to the choice of a
particular time-span.

In what sense is the human course a short one? Length is always
relative. Human life is short compared with the life of planets and
galaxies, long compared with that of fruit-flies and lightning flashes.
Standards of comparison have to be chosen for their relevance to
particular purposes. Weinberg's choice of a very long span is useful
enough in correcting the escalator model. That correction, however,
should not make him rebound from wild euphoria to equally wild
depression. The reason for this reaction is that he has chosen another
perspective which is just as unsuitable as the first for direct application to human purposes. It is true that notions like meaning and
purpose find no application in the first three cosmic minutes, or across
uncounted ages, or in the movement of particles, or in the collapse of

the galaxies, or at the surface of Betelgeuse, or indeed for most of the time at our own North Pole, because these notions only make sense in relation to organisms of a certain degree of complexity. I am deliberately not touching on divine purposes in this discussion, so as to keep things simple and to meet Monod and Weinberg on their own non-religious ground. But even if we brought divine purposes in, we should probably have to say that their relation to these inorganic goings on was mysterious to us. Teleological thinking simply does not help us in these fields, as it does in biology and above all in human affairs. But since these are anyway not the fields in which we live, or in which the purposes of any living things are deployed, they could not be the right place to look for that meaning which must consist essentially in a pattern related to such purposes.

Back to earth

If we drop our surprising ambition to figure as central actors on the cosmic stage, and return to our own field of terrestrial life, we shall find no shortage of purposes, many of them very demanding. We shall probably see the problem of meaning as chiefly one of harmonizing these purposes, and of understanding them well enough not to waste our lives on shadows. Among these purposes, those concerned with knowledge will indeed appear as important, and the sciences, physical and otherwise, as very serious fields of human endeavour. But the idea that they, or any narrow group of them, could furnish the whole purpose of human life will probably strike us as extremely strange. Since its effect is to tear the human faculties apart, divorcing intellect from feeling, spirit, action and bodily perception, it denies even to intellect itself most of the scope which it should naturally have. The anthropologist Colin Turnbull draws attention to the strange way in which our educational system, unlike many others, systematically divides the human faculties by educating each on its own and avoiding problems of integration. He points out:

> the need for all of us, whatever we are doing, to do it with the whole of our being and not just as an intellectual exercise or just to accomplish some physical or mechanical goal. . . . Good mechanics, like good craftsmen in any walk of life, put pride into their work, doing it with their whole being, with concern for others with whom, through their work, they are in contact.[4]

Occupations, scientific or otherwise, treated in this way need not, as he points out, either divide up an individual's own nature or split him off from those around him in the competitive isolation which is so frequent a feature of western education. They can help him instead to integrate all his powers in a balanced fulfilment – an aim which is, as he points out, amazingly absent from the theory and practice of our schooling, and especially from the current ideal of a scientist. Only in the last few decades has that ideal even begun to acquire an active component, as the notion of social responsibility has gradually, and against much opposition, begun to be grafted again on to the official concept of science. But to give play for that active component, scientists have, like Einstein, to see themselves as not only scientists, but responsible men and women whose business it is to weigh together whole ranges of human aims, among which the aims of the various sciences form only a part. Specialization must often be resisted, and thought on general subjects positively encouraged. There is no standing at all for the dogmatic idea that science can simply be treated as the only important activity, having won the race with all other human aims in a walkover.

The really startling thing about this idea, in the forms in which it is now put forward, is its unthinkingness. When people like H. G. Wells, and occasionally T. H. Huxley, used to make this kind of suggestion, they knew that it needed hard argument of the most varied kinds to support it. They saw the moral, political, psychological, logical and metaphysical difficulties, as well as a number of straight biological ones, and tried to meet each set strenuously in its own appropriate style. The heirs of this enterprise, by contrast, sitting comfortably on the status which has been provided for them, tend not to find any argument necessary. For them, this picture is the only possible one. The habitual conviction of the all-sufficiency of science looks to them like something, not just obvious, but itself scientifically established. It looks, in fact, as we have seen, like a part of the theory of evolution. It also serves them, however, as a religion in that it tells them what to venerate, indicating the supreme values available and justifying the sacrifice of all others to them. Since its basis is in fact not scientific at all but merely imaginative, it seems to be a fair question whether this faith should not be viewed simply as one religion among the others available. The reason why this now looks startling is because today science and religion are still often seen as in some sense polar opposites. It will help us, I think, to look carefully at the meaning of this opposition, and of some others related to it, in the next chapter.

12
Mixed antitheses

Something I owe to the soil that grew –
  More to the life that fed –
But most to Allah Who gave me two
  Separate sides to my head.

I would go without shirt or shoes
  Friends, tobacco or bread
Sooner than for an instant lose
  Either side of my head.

Rudyard Kipling, Kim, Chapter VIII

Balancing the world

I have been arguing that the contrast between science and religion is unluckily not as plain, nor the relation between them as simple, as is often supposed, and have been discussing some elements which can equally form part of either. Thoughtful scientists have often mentioned this problem, but a great many of their colleagues, and of the public generally, cling to the reassuringly simple opposition. What often seems to happen is that a great number of different antitheses are mixed up here, and used rather indiscriminately, as each happens to be convenient, to give colour to the idea of a general crusade of light against darkness. We could group them roughly like this:

1	science	v.	superstition partiality error magic wish-fulfilment dogmatism blind conformism childishness

2	common sense science rationalism logic	v.	intuition mysticism faith
	materialism	v.	idealism animism vitalism mind–body dualism commonsense agnosticism

3	hard	v.	soft
	progress	v.	tradition
	determinism	v.	free will
	mechanism	v.	teleology
	empiricism	v.	rationalism metaphysics
	scepticism	v.	credulity
	reason	v.	feeling or emotion
	objective	v.	subjective
	quantity	v.	quality
	physical science	v.	the humanities
	realism	v.	reverence
	specialism	v.	holism
	prose	v.	poetry
	male	v.	female
	clarity	v.	mystery

Shifting paradigms

A mental map based on this strange group of antitheses, a map which showed them all as roughly equivalent and was marked only with the general direction 'keep to the left', has for the last century usually been issued to English-speaking scientists with their first test-tube and has often gone with them to the grave. In spite of its wild incoherence, it still has great influence, though at least two recent developments within science itself have lately shaken it, and more are to be expected. The first shock is the series of changes whereby modern physics now shows indeterminacy as lying near the centre of causation, and solid matter as dissolving, on inspection, into non-solid energy. This is a severe upset to the crucial notions of mechanism and determinism. What perhaps cuts deepest, however, is something symbolic which looks more superficial and which would not matter at all if people were really only interested in facts and not in drama. It is the disturbance to the notion of 'hardness', a metaphor whose application is entirely mysterious, but which has somehow served to keep the whole left-hand column together.

At present, this change results in a flow of popular books such as *The Tao of Physics* by Fritdjof Capra and *The Dancing Wu Li Masters* by Gary Zukav,[1] which suggest that energy is spirit, and that what modern physics teaches is, give or take a mantra or two, very much what Zen masters and Hindu sages have been saying for centuries, or possibly millennia. Whatever else may be thought about this, it does at least point to the need to look again at our list of antitheses. On the face of things, these books do draw attention to the arbitrary narrow-mindedness which has been imposed on scientists, and call for science to look outward, though at times they also seem to convey the opposite message: science, especially physics, is already far more spiritual, and therefore more all-sufficient, than we have so far supposed. At least, however, the traditional set of antitheses is broken up. Serious physicists seem at present more aware than many biologists of its confusions and inadequacies. David Bohm's comment, extracts from which we saw earlier, deserves now to be quoted more fully:

At the end of the nineteenth century, physicists widely believed that classical physics gave the general outlines of a complete mechanical explanation of the universe. Since then, relativity and quantum theory have overturned such notions altogether. It is now clear that no mechanical explanation is available, not for the fundamental particles which constitute all matter, inanimate and animate, nor for the cosmos as a whole (e.g. it is now widely accepted among cosmologists that in 'black holes' there is a singularity, near which all customary notions of causally ordered law break down). So we are now in the strange position that whereas physicists are implying that, fundamentally and in its totality, inanimate matter is not mechanical, molecular biologists are saying that whenever matter is organized so as to be alive, it is completely mechanical.

Of course, molecular biologists generally ignore the implications of physics, except when these implications support their own position. In this connection, it might be appropriate for them to consider that the nineteenth-century view of physics was enormously more comprehensively and accurately tested than is now possible for the current views of molecular biology. Despite this, classical physics was swept aside and overturned, being retained only as a simplification and an approximation valid in a certain limited domain. Is it not likely that modern molecular biology will sooner or later undergo a similar fate?

What is needed for unrestricted objectivity is a certain tentative and exploratory quality of mind that is free of final conclusions. [Without this, there is an] ever-present danger that knowledge in broad and deep fields may give rise to the sort of 'hubris' described above, in which there is an unquestioned belief in the complete validity of current forms of thinking. . . . If [this] is allowed to continue in science, this latter will in all probability eventually suffer the sort of decline of influence which has already befallen the religious view of the world. Indeed, there are already signs of such a trend.[2]

The second shock was delivered by recent discoveries about the functions of brain hemispheres. In its early days, this was often read, in a way which is itself a notable indicator of the underlying dramas expected, as a story about the 'dominance' of one hemisphere, namely of course the calculating, articulate, scientific one, over the other, which was intuitive, humble and not really very distinctively human. Further research, however, has steadily shown more and more serious functions for the right-hand hemisphere, and has led increasingly to the acceptance of Kipling's picture expressed at the beginning of this chapter, where it is utterly vital to have, and to keep in balance, the two separate sides of one's head. The idea of the ruling hemisphere had been just one more version of a simple but very powerful hierarchical view of mental function which long dominated neurology, and which Peter Reynolds, the comparative ethologist, has lately christened 'the Victorian brain'.[3] This showed brain evolution dramatically as a series of successive conquests, in which at each level of life a new brain area and its faculties came in to rule the rest, culminating in man and the final victory of the cerebral cortex, or some specially splendid part of it. To keep this dominance order clear, functions were neatly confined to particular structures, and the belief that *homo sapiens* possessed not just a better cortex but entirely distinct organs to carry his higher faculties was at first hotly defended by Owen against Huxley. Detailed neurological work has, however, worn away almost every aspect of this seductive picture. As Stephen Walker, a neurological psychologist, says,

One still has a sense of regret that this charming and convincing tale must be discarded. The weight of evidence is now if anything more in favour of the unhelpful suggestion . . . that all the fundamental parts of the vertebrate brain were present very early on, and can be observed in lampreys.[4]

Moreover, new developments do not at all follow the simple pattern of conquest and takeover. Functions are neither handed over wholesale to grander organs nor fully determined by them; they seem to involve very complex interactions between wide ranges of brain areas, in which it is seldom safe to say either that any one area takes no part, or that any one dominates or 'rules' any others. No doubt each makes its own distinctive contribution, to which adjectives like 'higher' might sometimes usefully be applied, but the only social metaphor which seems appropriate for these transactions is co-operation. The brain, in short, works as a whole, and our understanding of it has been very much held back by the fact that, as Walker remarks, 'there is a tendency to want to appoint some brain division as "in charge" of all the others, and this sets the stage for phylogenetic takeovers of the executive position.'

Brain evolution, in short, is not a simple success story establishing the right of all left-hand members in our antitheses to subdue their partners. Since the members of the two sets are in any case such a mixed lot as to make this wholesale arrangement impossible, we had better look at them separately on their merits.

Finding the right enemy

Which among these antitheses are really the ones we need, which of them give clear ground for a crusade? The ones in the first group seem the most promising for crusaders. In them science stands opposed to something undoubtedly bad. But in these cases it is certainly not the only opponent of the evils in question. Superstition and the rest find their opposites in clear thinking generally, and a particular superstition is as likely to be corrected by history or logic or common sense as by one of the physical sciences. The second group deals in ideas which are more ambitious, more interesting, but also much more puzzling, because we at once need definitions of the terms involved, and cannot easily give them without falling into confusion. The odd tendency of both rationalism and common sense to jump the central barrier is only one indication of the difficulties. In the third group, we have contrasts which are a good deal clearer. But they do not seem to provide material at all suitable for a crusade. They describe pairs of complementary elements in life and thought, both members of which are equally necessary, and indeed could scarcely be identified except in relation to each other as parts of a whole. We no longer want that truculent little 'v.' to divide them. They go very well together, and crusaders must avoid trying to set them at loggerheads. Thus it does not matter here that 'reason' appears on both sides; we no longer want to reduce all these contrasts to a single underlying shape. The lines of division cross each other. Different distinctions are needed for different purposes.

How hard it is to relate these various antitheses clearly can be seen in Bertrand Russell's very interesting and influential paper 'Mysticism and logic'. Russell's main enterprise here is an admirable attempt to move the whole debate into our group 3, to show apparently warring elements as both necessary and complementary:

> Metaphysics, or the attempt to conceive the world as a whole by means of thought, has been developed, from the first, by the union and conflict of two very different human impulses, the one urging men towards mysticism, the other urging them towards science. . . . In Hume, for instance, the scientific impulse reigns quite unchecked, while in Blake a strong hostility to science co-exists with profound mystic insight. But the greatest men who have been philosophers have felt the need both of science and of mysticism; the attempt to harmonize the two was what made their life, and what always must, for all its arduous uncertainty, make philosophy, to some minds, a greater thing than either science or religion. . . . Mysticism, is, in essence, little more than a certain intensity and depth of feeling in regard to what is believed about the universe. . . . Mysticism is to be commended as an attitude towards life, not as a creed about the world. The metaphysical creed, I shall maintain, is a mistaken outcome of the emotion, although this emotion, as colouring all other thoughts and feelings, is the inspirer of whatever is best in Man. Even the cautious and patient investigation of truth by science, which seems the very antithesis of the mystic's swift certainty, may be fostered and nourished by that very spirit of reverence in which mysticism lives and moves.[5]

Russell has got a lot of things right here. He has 'got in', as they say, many items from the right-hand column of our antitheses in legitimate relation to science. He has got in emotion and poetry, indeed he has got in Blake, with his criticisms of Newton. He sees that emotion is so far from being an opponent of science, or a menace to it, that emotion of a suitable kind is necessary for science, and that part of that emotion can quite properly be called 'reverence'. He sees that something of the sort is necessary for metaphysics too.

The word metaphysics here is not of course used in the abusive sense to mean mere empty vapouring. It is used in its proper sense of very general conceptual enquiry, covering such central topics as the relation of mind and matter, free will and necessity, meaning, truth and the possibility of knowledge, all in an attempt (as Russell rightly says) to make sense of the world as a whole. In this sense, naturally, views like materialism and empiricism, and also sceptical enquiries like those of Hume, Ayer and Popper are themselves part of metaphysics just as much as what they oppose or enquire into. When A. J. Ayer began his book *Language, Truth and Logic*[6] with a chapter called 'The elimination of metaphysics', and went on to explain that the word was for him virtually equivalent to 'nonsense', he was, in any ordinary sense of that word, simply doing metaphysics himself – expounding one theory of meaning among many others. Empty vapouring is *bad* metaphysics. There is a lot of it about, but it cannot make the study unnecessary.

Russell, who had the advantage of having started his philosophical life as a disciple of Hegel, was not tempted, as Hume and his disciples were, to suppose that good metaphysics merely meant cutting down one's thoughts on such topics to a minimum. He knew that, far from that, even highly constructive metaphysicians like Plato and Heraclitus, Leibnitz and Hegel often had something very important to say, especially about mathematics. Yet he was now a convert to empiricism, and he wanted to set limits on the thought-architecture of these bold rationalists. His solution was, on the whole, to concentrate on the emotional function of this large-scale, constructive metaphysics, and on the intellectual function of science and of more sceptical philosophy. Thus mystical, constructive metaphysics was to supply the heart of the world-grasping enterprise, while science supplied the head.

The many-sidedness of science

This is a bold and ingenious idea, but something has gone wrong with it. He has fitted the head of one kind of enquiry on to the heart of another. Constructive metaphysics has its own thoughts, and science its own motives. If the word *science* means what it seems to mean here – primarily the search for particular facts – then it is powered emotionally by the familiar motive of detailed curiosity. If it means the building of those facts into a harmonious, satisfying system, then it draws upon a different motive, the desire for intellectual order; which is also the motive for metaphysical endeavour. Without this unifying urge, science would be nothing but mindless, meaningless collecting. At the quite ordinary scientific level, before any question of mystically contemplating the whole comes in, the system-building tendency, with its aesthetic criteria of elegance and order, is an essential part of every science, continually shaping the scrappy data into usable patterns. Scientific hypotheses are not generated by randomizers, nor do they grow on trees, but on the branches of these ever-expanding thought systems.

This is why the sciences continually go beyond everybody's direct experience, and do so in directions that quickly diverge from that of common sense, which has more modest systems of its own. And because isolated systems are always incomplete and can conflict with each other, inevitably in the end they require metaphysics, 'the attempt to conceive the world as a whole', to harmonize them.

To what are interestingly called *lay* people, however, these intellectual constructions present problems of belief which are often quite as difficult as those of religion, and which can call for equally strenuous efforts of faith. This happens at present over relativity, over the size and expansion of the universe, over quantum mechanics, over evolution and many other matters. Believers are – perhaps quite properly – expected to bow to the mystery, admit the inadequacy of their faculties, and accept paradoxes. If a mystical sense of reverence is, as Russell suggested, the right response to the vast and incomprehensible universe, then science itself requires it, since it leads us on directly to this situation. It cannot therefore be right to call mysticism and science, as Russell does, two distinct, co-ordinate 'human impulses'. Mysticism is a range of human faculties; physical science, a range of enquiries which can, at times, call these faculties into action. But long before it does so, it has passed the limits of common sense, transcended experience and begun to ask for faith.

At this stage, there is often a real problem about what kind of thinking is going on, and whether it ought to be stopped. If, for instance, we ask whether the universe is finite, are we still talking about anything at all? If so, do we know what it is? The most general concepts used by any science – concepts like life, time, space, law, energy – raise serious headaches, affecting their use in actual problems. To resolve these, however, we often need not more facts but a better way of fitting these concepts into their neighbours, of stating the wider problems which surround them, of 'conceiving the world as a whole'. Science quite properly calls on the whole range of our cognitive faculties, but it is not alone in doing so, nor can it define their whole aim. It is a part of our attempt to understand the universe, not the whole of it. It opens into metaphysics.

13
Science, scepticism and awe

I do not know what I may appear to the world, but to myself I seem to have been only a boy playing on the sea-shore, and diverting myself in now and then finding a smoother pebble or a prettier shell than ordinary, whilst the great ocean of truth lay all undiscovered before me.

Isaac Newton

Science as a part of life

Where does this glance at Russell's diagnosis take us? We have been trying to bring some order into the chaotic mix of antitheses from which we started, using first the approach which Russell suggests. This approach gives us some legitimate footing for the emotional elements on the right-hand of our columns, but not yet for the cognitive ones. It shows emotion, reverence, poetry and the sense of mystery, not as opponents of science, but as at least its equals, elements just as necessary for a balanced intellectual life, and perhaps more necessary for life as a whole. In view of the remarks about Blake, this will also give a standing to the humanities, not as illicit, upstart competitors with science, but as its distinct and equal colleagues. It gives a possibility of fitting science realistically into the rest of life, reminding us what other parts that life must have. (Russell did not greatly stress this reminder because in his day the boot was still on the other foot; humanists were the ones who needed reminding of the importance of science. No doubt they often still do. But their resolute blindness is now more than equalled by that of their opponents.)

What Russell does not manage to do is to find an adequate place for the wandering cognitive elements which appear in the right-hand columns, notably rationalism, common sense and metaphysics. He seems inclined to count everything cognitive except philosophy as science. This neglects not only such disciplines as history, but also certain important contrasts which should really appear on the left-hand side of the barrier – differences within our cognitive faculties themselves, which make the notion of science a very complex one. Russell writes here as if there were no difference between the various sciences, and as if science, common sense and experience were virtually the same thing – a kind of downright everyday truthfulness about the facts, straightforwardly opposed to the extravagant Hegelian metaphysics which flows from treating mystical emotion as a source of knowledge. Yet in his earlier book *The Problems of Philosophy* he had pointed out the gulf between them.[1] Our common-sense beliefs go far beyond our own individual experience, and are often at odds with it. And the fully developed sciences tell a quite different story from both. Much hard conceptual plumbing is needed if we are to connect them all in any sort of a watertight manner. Russell's mention of Hume here as someone in whom 'the scientific impulse reigns quite unchecked' shows strikingly how far he had for the moment forgotten this kind of difficulty. Hume was no less deeply sceptical about physical science than he was about every other intellectual enterprise. Because he was so determined an empiricist, so resolute to accept nothing except individual experience, he thought the idea of causal necessity and the regularity of nature extremely fishy, and sharply criticized his predecessor Locke's credulity about it. 'If we believe that fire warms, or water refreshes, it is only because it costs us too much pains to think otherwise.'[2] British empiricism did not move from this sceptical position towards any real acceptance of modern science until Mill wrote his *Logic*. This still left further difficulties, which Russell himself did a great deal to remove. But there is a formidable pile of them left today, providing work for anyone (scientist or philosopher) who wants to understand what the sciences are really doing, and to see how to deal with their conflicts. Within the notion of science itself there are large, unresolved clashes, notably between the idea that it is simply a vast memory store, a register of facts, and the quite different one that it is an intellectual system constructed by reasoning as a means to understanding the universe. These problems are of course no discredit to science. But they are a real obstacle to inscribing its name on a banner as a simple sign to fight under.

On having faith in reason

These divisions bring us to another key case, rationalism. This means confidence in reason; people's attitude to it naturally depends on what reason is supposed to be opposing at the time. When the opposite is superstition or some other member of our first right-hand column, there is no problem; all intellectuals are supposed to be united against it. But there is also the much less simple situation in which reason is opposed to experience – where people's perceptions seem not to accord with what they believe must be true, as for instance over the size of the stars or the shape of the earth or the solidity of matter. Science is by no means always on the side of experience here, as is plain from these examples, and still plainer when unexpected results are dismissed as experimental error, or in cases like parapsychology where scientists unite to refuse to look at certain groups of data at all. This may be perfectly reasonable. But the point we have to notice about it here is the strong faith which it testifies in a general, theoretical, *a priori* view of the universe.

Perhaps some such faith is an intellectual necessity. In that case, the important thing seems to be not to take it for granted, but to be conscious of it, to distinguish its various elements, and to see on what grounds we can choose between them when there are alternatives. Moderate rationalism – a certain degree of confidence in reasoning against experience – can be perfectly rational. It need not commit us, as the stronger rationalism of Plato and Hegel does, to regarding the world of experience as in any way unreal or delusive. But what it does mean is that we cannot defend our theories by treating them simply as if they were matters of direct experience. They depend also on faith, on a choice about how to regard the universe. It must follow, again, that faith is not just something to be got rid of, but something to be rightly directed.

Sceptical difficulties

This may worry some readers. Have we really a right to trust our faculties and assume that the universe they show us is as a whole lawful and regular enough to allow reason to be used on it? Yes, we surely do. Philosophical sceptics, if they really urge us to drop this bad habit of faith, are still relying on these faculties, but using them for an illicit kind of moral blackmail. They trade on the moral prestige which rightly belongs to selective, discriminating scepticism, to care and caution in distinguishing good from bad grounds for belief. This moral prestige cannot be extended to the undiscriminating, universal kind, which would stop us drawing any such distinctions at all. Sometimes, of course, philosophical sceptics are only talking about rules for the convenient use of words, as when they deliberately narrow the use of terms like 'knowledge'. And this kind of modest move can be useful. But something far more ambitious than this is happening when they put on their own drama, the drama which is played for all it will pull in the concluding chapter to the first volume of Hume's *Treatise*. Here the sceptical hero stands exalted as Odysseus, the only man strong enough to resist the siren-song of normal evidence and know that belief is never really justified. (He doesn't actually *disbelieve*, but he knows that he only believes because it would cost him too much pains to do otherwise. Others stop their ears; they will not accept this painful truth.) This scene draws its moral force from its resemblance to one where some particular false proposition is presented for acceptance, perhaps enforced by threats, for instance in the trial of Galileo. Nothing of this kind is actually happening over these attempts to question in some vast and general way the entire practice of belief. What is going on is either just a modest negotiation about the convenient use of concepts – which would call for no special heroism – or it is a demonstration in support of a particular moral position, namely, that incredulousness is in itself a virtue and credulity a vice. It is always more blessed to disbelieve than to believe.

The colours which Hume slaps on here make it impossible to suppose that he is only engaged in a quiet bit of conceptual plumbing. His moral indignation and alarm are evident. And they are quite in place if they are understood – as in practice they mostly are – as calling for *selective* scepticism, for a readiness to question unexamined dogmas. But if this is inflated into genuinely undiscriminating disbelief, questions can have no answers, and the act of questioning itself becomes fraudulent and meaningless.

The reader will notice that I see this as one more situation where the essential thing is to spot the drama, grasp its meaning and disentangle it from the real argument. Monomania on my part is one possible explanation, but another is that there is something in what I say. This kind of thing does, I suspect, flourish particularly easily in the work of writers who are letting it be known that they are particularly down-to-earth, unconventional and non-religious. Drama is as likely to be present in them as in any other kind of writer, and is, as I have said, in itself perfectly legitimate. But it will not be so easily noticed and allowed for as it is where the work is known to be imaginative and metaphysical. Hume's work shows this, and also another feature which seems to be common, namely the use of a drama which was suitable in his own day, but becomes less so later, yet still continues to play to full houses under its own emotional steam. In Hume's time, professed, chronic unbelievers (especially in religion) were rare. The vices endemic to professed, chronic believers, such as complacency, lazy-mindedness and easy shockability, were dominant. When, however, unbelievers began to grow more common, they in their turn naturally revealed their own characteristic vices, such as arrogance, perversity and self-dramatization. At first, no doubt, it is a gain to counter the vices typical of age with those of youth. But later this stops being half so obviously true, and to settle the balance would call for a direct moral argument. It cannot be done in Hume's way, as a spin-off from a very abstract metaphysical enquiry. Moreover, once disbelief itself becomes fashionable, one can get the benefit of both sets of vices together, not only in the same epoch but in the same person. Narrow-minded, conformist sceptics and immoralists are now a standard issue.

Both sets of vices are equally distracting and dangerous. There is, I suggest, no possibility of properly calling either credulity or incredulity in themselves good or bad. There is no short cut; we need to believe and disbelieve the right things. Since disbelief, as much as belief, is a positive, chosen attitude, parsimony cannot settle the matter. Neither belief nor disbelief can be bought wholesale, as a general policy. We simply have to assess particular propositions on their merits.

A much more limited kind of scepticism, which was particularly important to Russell, is logical atomism. This is the view that all truths are particular truths. Out of these, general theories may be constructed, but quite general prepositions about the universe as a whole are vacuous. Thus Russell, reacting sharply against the bold Hegelian view that the universe was essentially one, ruled (with equal boldness) that the very notion of a universe was an illicit one:

> I believe that conception of 'the universe' to be, as its etymology indicates, a mere relic of pre-Copernican astronomy. . . . The apparent oneness of the world is an undiscussed postulate of most metaphysics . . . [but really] the apparent oneness of the world is merely the oneness of what is seen by a single spectator or apprehended by a single mind.[3]

This principle would veto all talk about the universe as a whole, and prevent our expressing any general view of it, such as a confidence that it is regular. Logical atomism is, in fact, a specialized form of scepticism, but it is one to which we need not bow, for it rests on a confusion. The particular propositions which it treats as ultimate could not have been formed without the framework of wider conceptual schemes which serves as their background and provides their terms. As Wittgenstein saw, particular propositions cannot always be prior to general ones. Both are elements in language, which is itself an element in our whole system of behaviour.[4] In a crucial sense, the whole is always prior to its parts. And unquestionably this kind of belief in a law-abiding universe – which is a real belief, not just a policy – is a precondition of any possible physical science.

Awe, reverence and mystery

In what spirit, then, is it rational for a scientist to confront the universe in which he has this kind of confidence? Julian Huxley, the thoughtful zoologist who was Thomas Henry's grandson, answered without hesitation that this spirit was bound to be a religious one, simply because of the situation of our species as a tiny part of it. In man, he says,

> for the first time life becomes aware of something more than a set of events; it becomes aware of a system of powers operating in events. . . . Man frames his own idea of these powers. . . . We call it religious when on the one hand it involves some recognition of powers operating so as to underlie the general operation of the world, and, on the other hand, when it involves the emotions.[5]

In such a relation, awe and reverence are (he insists) entirely appropriate emotions, and an investigator who lacks them will make a bad scientist. Russell – of course no less atheistic – made a similar remark, though he did not use the word 'religion' so widely:

> In religion, and in every deeply serious view of the world and of human destiny, there is an element of submission, a realization of the limits of human power, which is somewhat lacking in the modern world, with its quick material successes, and its insolent belief in the boundless possibilities of progress. 'He that loveth his life shall lose it', and there is danger lest, through a too confident love of life, life itself should lose much of what gives it its highest worth. The submission which religion inculcates in action is essentially the same in spirit as that which science teaches in thought.[6]

Similarly Dobzhansky:

> Rejecting vitalism in no way conflicts with what Albert Schweitzer has called 'reverence for life.' Man's conscience, the existence of life, and indeed of the universe itself, all are parts of the *mysterium tremendum*. . . . There is no more succinct, and at the same time accurate, statement of the distinctive quality of human nature than that of Dostoevsky; 'Man needs the unfathomable and the infinite just as much as he does the small

planet which he inhabits'. . . . In every known human society . . . peoples have arrived at some system of religious views concerning the meaning and the proper conduct of their lives. . . . Religion enables human beings to make peace with themselves and with the formidable and mysterious universe into which they are flung by some power greater than themselves.[7]

This attitude owes a good deal to the fact that Dobzhansky, like Einstein and Newton, is the kind of scientist who emphasizes the inevitable slightness of the whole scientific achievement and its absurd disproportion to the vastness of what there is to be known, rather than the kind who claims (like Wilson) that the job is nearly finished, or that, as Francis Crick puts it,

While a scientist is sobered by the economic and political problems he sees all around him, he is possessed of *an almost boundless optimism concerning his ability to forge a wholly new set of beliefs*, solidly based on both theory and experiment, by a careful study of the world around him and, ultimately, of himself and other human beings. . . . The feeling is that within a few generations we shall have got to the heart of the matter. (my italics)[8]

The matter in question is 'the intricacies of the brain' and its relation to the mind. But Crick is equally cheerful about the whole mind–body problem and a wide range of questions which surround it including 'major efforts to improve the nature of man himself'.[9] Readers will inevitably tend to divide themselves here into those who think that the difference between these two groups of scientists is due to the startling scientific progress made in the decade or two between their times of writing, and those who explain it, more simply, by a sharp decline in the quality of scientific education. The point I am currently making about the idea of 'the universe' as a whole is that, if one means by it not much more than is already described in scientific books, one is less likely to be deeply impressed with its vastness and mystery than if one regards those books as small mirrors reflecting only parts of its more superficial aspects.

Is it in order for Dobzhansky and Huxley to describe their world-view as religious, or even as a religion? It is obviously not a religion in the full sense, if that is taken to mean that a recruit can put it down in the appropriate column of his army form and expect suitable provision for worship. But, as I suggested at the outset, some of the elements combined in Christianity and its more familiar alternatives seem to be dispersing, and many other religions never combined them all in the first place. In their original forms, Buddhism had no god and Judaism no doctrine of immortality. Stoicism, which also lacked both and had no ritual either, clearly served most of the functions of a religion for its followers. So does Marxism, which has a good deal in common with the evolutionist faith.

William James, in some thoughtful remarks about the outer limits of the term, concluded that an attitude could usefully be called religious so long as it was one directed to the world as a whole, 'about which there is something solemn, serious and tender'.[10] It must also be an attitude of acceptance, not rejection, and an acceptance which is not grudging but enthusiastic. This acceptance rests on 'belief that there is an unseen order', and flows from 'that fundamental mystery of religious experience, the satisfaction found in absolute surrender to the larger power', a surrender which of course is not just masochistic, but based on the sense that all things work together for good. Because this kind of attitude has had such a bad press in western thought since the eighteenth century, James has to spend a great deal of his book pointing out that it will not do for empiricists, of all people, to dismiss so potent an element in life unexamined. Empiricism, he says, demands that we look at a range of experience seriously and open-mindedly, and consider what is the best way to describe it, not that we define it in advance in ways designed to outlaw alternative descriptions, or forms of it which we find inconvenient.

Two ways of exalting evolution

In this book I have of course not tried to duplicate James's work, but a particular aspect of it is of great interest here, namely the path by which scientists, merely by being scientists, can find themselves using and resting in an attitude which is in a plain sense religious. The intellectual attitude necessary for science, if given its full scope and not reduced artificially to a mere mindless tic for collecting, is continuous with a typically religious view of the physical world. This is one of the varieties of religious experience. The sense of a sharp opposition here is misleading. When this fact is noticed, however, very fishy conclusions are sometimes drawn from it, which tend to produce the bizarre and sometimes monstrous prophecies we have seen. Scientists who see that they are in some sense neighbours of religion are sometimes moved, not to an exploration of relations and shared interests, but to the hope of loot and plunder. Julian Huxley often notes with exasperation that orthodox religion, of a kind which he himself finds pointless, seems still to retain its force, while science, even when believed, has much less influence. He wants a transfer of spiritual assets. Edward O. Wilson, noting the same phenomenon, wastes no time complaining but spits on his palms to set the matter right:

> The time has come to ask: Does a way exist to divert the power of religion into the service of the great new enterprise that lays bare the sources of that power? . . . Make no mistake about the power of scientific materialism. It presents the human mind with an alternative mythology that until now has always, point for point in zones of conflict, defeated traditional religion. Its narrative form is the epic, the evolution of the universe from the big bang.[11]

The reasoning that because something is strong it deserves to become stronger is noteworthy. Wilson's attitude here may look superficially like Dobzhansky's, but it is really quite different. Dobzhansky is expressing his own highly complex faith, and is much concerned with its difficulties. Wilson, in a manner all too familiar to Christians, is asking 'what faith does the age require?' He is in no doubt about the answer, which he gives in the conclusion of *On Human Nature*:

> The true Promethean spirit of science . . . constructs the mythology of scientific materialism, guided by the corrective devices of the scientific method, *addressed with precise and deliberately affective appeal* to the deepest needs of human nature, and kept strong by the *blind hopes* that the journey on which we are now embarked will be farther and better than the one just completed. (my italics)[12]

(It is interesting that the hopes are blind.) He is chiefly concerned with how best to make converts. Dobzhansky, being deeply interested in other people's faiths and the problems which surround them, recognizes at once the religious elements in his own position, and, drawing on his background in Russian Orthodox Christianity, maps out the various religious and non-religious paths which neighbour his own, considering them as real options. For Wilson the word 'religion' seems to be little more than the banner of an alien tribe, whose assets are to be raided. He seldom mentions any manifestation of religion which is not openly crude and contemptible. Dobzhansky sees that science and religion cannot, properly speaking, be in competition: 'Science and religion deal with different aspects of existence. If one dares to overschematize for the sake of clarity, one may say that these are the aspect of fact and the aspect of meaning.'[13] He deals with many local conflicts between views on both sides, but aims steadily to bring both into focus together. Wilson never doubts either that there is direct competition or that it has been won, since science (in the form of sociobiology) has 'explained' religion, while religion cannot explain science.[14] This is an amazingly confused position. Causal explanation (which is the only kind offered) is not relevant to the value of the thing explained, as can be seen by thinking about the parallel case of a possible causal explanation of mathematics or of science itself. Moreover, this causal explanation of religion is not actually provided; it is only promised and loosely sketched as a project. It consists of some familiar shaky speculations about the way in which various religions might help the survival of tribes professing them, plus the *a priori* ruling that not only religion in general, but also a preference for a particular kind of religion, is genetically determined. What Wilson is really trying to do is to account for the existence and power of religion, on the uncriticized assumption that its content is nothing but a load of humbug. Some people approach questions about the existence and power of sociobiology in the same spirit. In neither case does this seem to be a useful way to understand the phenomenon.

One last contrast: Dobzhansky really does understand the difference between ideals and predictions, and Wilson does not. Prophets can fairly deal in both these wares, but it is vital that they should grasp the distinction. Predictions get their support from factual evidence. Ideals get theirs from considerations of value. From its outset, the Wellsian tradition of prophecy, centring on a distorted, emotive notion of 'science', has mixed these methods. It has tended to represent its own chosen conception of the future as obligatory because it was inevitable, and vice versa. The roots of this bad habit go back to Nietzsche, who first suggested answering the question 'why should we do this?' by saying 'because the future calls for it'. Nietzsche's main point was that this is a better answer than 'because we have always done it in the past'. Even if this is true – which is none too obvious – neither option is any substitute for relevant reasons.

14

The service of self and the service of Kali

Though Nature, red in tooth and claw
  With ravin, shrieked against his creed . . .

Are God and Nature then at strife
  That Nature lends such evil dreams?
  So careful of the type she seems,
So careless of the single life;

'So careful of the type?' but no
  From scarped cliff and quarried stone
  She cries, 'A thousand types are gone;
I care for nothing; all shall go.'
                    Alfred Lord Tennyson, *In Memoriam*, LV–LVI

Nature's redness and the abuse of common speech

We move on now from strange beliefs based on optimistic distortions
of evolutionary theory to ones based on pessimistic distortions, from
Lamarck's escalator to nature red in tooth and claw. Are we then still
in realms which ought to be called religious at all? Certainly this is a
gloomy and alarming cult. But it is still one celebrated with powerful
incantations, such as Tennyson's and that of M. T. Ghiselin (quoted
on pp. 2–3 and to be looked at again shortly). As we have already seen,
even the cosmic escalator, when set against a sufficiently vast and
disheartening backdrop, can give a deeply gloomy impression. Yet
the drama to which this picture contributes is certainly spiritually
ambitious enough to constitute a faith and in some sense a religion.
We need to notice here the general place of gloomy elements in

religions. Most of the Greek and Roman deities were sometimes deeply destructive, and some – Hecate, Nemesis, Pluto – dealt with death as their main function. Still more interesting is the Hindu trinity of Brahma, Vishnu and Siva – Creator, Preserver and Destroyer. Siva, and still more his wife Kali, stand for death. And death is indeed a most necessary balance to the rich fertility that flows from the first two members. In the context of the whole, these deities supply a grave and becoming element. When, however, they are worshipped on their own, some very odd activity and even odder motivation tend to be involved. Thugs serve the goddess by ritual murder of strangers. Still more remarkably, ecstatic devotees perish by throwing themselves under the car of Jagarnath.

That exaltation of pure destruction seems to me to be the main inspiration of Ghiselin's hymn to egoism and of other passages like it. This is a paradoxical suggestion, since in theory these passages celebrate an all-conquering urge to self-preservation. The emphasis in them, however, is never on the delights of the life which is to be preserved. It is all on an uncompromising determination to ditch all competitors. The mood celebrated is one of total destructive callousness. Tennyson and Ghiselin differ, however, about who owns this mood. For Tennyson it is still the figure of personified nature. Since God is still present, this shows us a kind of Huxleyan cosmic war in which another mood is still contending against this one. Ghiselin, by contrast, makes the mood entirely universal and uses no personification. He attributes it directly to all organisms.

Since most organisms are plants, which do not have motives, this seems strange. But in any case sociobiologists say plainly that they are not actually talking about motives at all. When they use words which are the ordinary names of motives, they officially do so with a quite different and technical meaning. This equivocation makes possible a chronic, pervasive play upon words. A colourful, familiar psychological myth is conveyed through the everyday meanings, and from time to time endorsed in unmistakable terms by the author – as it is here – without needing any actual discussion or support, because officially nothing but a theory in population genetics is on sale.

Trouble centres on the word *selfish*. For sociobiologists, this word is officially not the name of a motive at all, but a term used to describe a complicated, highly abstract and unfamiliar causal property – the tendency to maximize one's own gene representation in future generations. This is much like using the word *cruelty* to describe all behaviour which will cause suffering to anyone else in any future generation, or the word *sloth* to describe all that which will fail to affect them. Why such a word should ever have been chosen, if no reference to real selfishness was meant, is hard to imagine. Similar senses, however, are also given to the equally unsuitable motive-words, 'spite' and 'altruism'.

Now clumsy and ill-chosen scientific terms do not do much harm where their use is segregated from ordinary discourse. But this is not such a field. And there is in any case one kind of situation where they cannot be harmless, namely where their everyday sense also applies, and gives a common, familiar meaning with important consequences. The dangers of this situation are of course multiplied when a wide audience is being addressed. And it happens that the claim to detect ordinary, literal selfishness as an underlying motive, vitiating claims to other and better motives, is just such an everyday move. Its consequences are necessarily important, because it is so often used to justify retaliation. The fact that 'selfishness' in its ordinary sense is not just the name of a motive but of a fault naturally makes things much worse. To widen the imputation of selfishness is to alter people's view of the human race. This widening had of course already been deliberately undertaken by various thinkers who have developed theories of psychological egoism, and had been given a special political function by Hobbes and his followers in social-contract theory. People in society were then held not to have any motive in their interactions other than self-interest. If this bizarre story had been true, the notion of selfishness could never have arisen. Had regard for others really been impossible, there could have been no word for failing to have it. And it needs to be stressed that the word 'selfish' in its normal use is essentially a *negative* word. It means a shortage of this normal regard for others. Calling somebody selfish simply does not mean that they are prudent or successfully self-preserving. It merely says that they are exceptional – and faulty – in having too little care for anybody else.

Accordingly, egoist writers cannot properly use the term 'selfish' at all. Their theory excludes it. This is so obvious that usually they do not make this mistake. There is, however, a temptation to cheat by retaining it, because this makes possible the use of egoism to justify retributive bloody-mindedness based on a low opinion of our fellow-men. Egoist cheats enquire why we should be expected to bother about the rest of the human race, which has been proved guilty of the sin of selfishness? They warn anyone who is still rash enough to be unselfish that they are out on a limb and should quickly fall in line with the already universal tendency.

Various struggles for various existences

The absurdity of this talk has of course often been pointed out, and no one has any excuse for again attempting today to foist it on a long-suffering public. Historical chance, however, has favoured it by entangling it twice with apparently reputable scientific views. The first time this happened was in economics, when the early political economists conceived the idea that enlightened self-interest was the best path to promoting the interests of all, and called for commercial free enterprise unshackled by any restraints imposed to protect its victims. The second time was over evolution. This happened quite independently of Darwin. Tennyson published *In Memoriam* in 1850. Malthus had published his *Essay on Population* in 1798. The *Origin of Species* did not come out till 1859. Many others besides Darwin could see the drama implicit in the idea of a struggle for existence, and could project it loosely from the field of chaotic human life in a disturbed and rapidly changing society on to the vast, vague background of organic life generally. Where Darwin's invaluable special insight came in was in also grasping the differences between these fields. This released his imagination to work realistically in the biological one, and to work out in detail the way in which natural selection could be seen as a constructive force. Most other theorists oscillated in an uncontrolled way between the two fields, assuming what suited them about biology to make the points they wanted to make about society at the time.

Here again, of course, the dominant figure was Herbert Spencer, who had no hesitation at all about this proceeding. With only the most casual acquaintance with biology he promoted his notion of the 'survival of the fittest' as a social ideal. This had enormous effect, above all in the United States, where he outsold every other philosopher in his day. Two examples of the kind of thing which resulted must suffice; we are all too familiar with it still. Both come from direct disciples of Spencer's in America:

> The millionaires are a product of natural selection, acting on the whole body of men to pick out those who can meet the requirement of certain work to be done. . . . It is because they are thus selected that wealth – both their own and that entrusted to them – aggregates under their hands. . . . They may fairly be regarded as the naturally selected agents of society for certain work. They get high wages and live in luxury, but the bargain is a good one for society. There is the intensest competition for their place and occupation. This assures us that all who are competent for this function will be employed in it, so that the cost of it will be reduced to the lowest terms.[1]

And again, with a sharp illumination of the fatalistic aspect, Richard Hofstadter in his admirable analysis of Social Darwinism observes how:

acceptance of the Spencerian philosophy brought about a paralysis of the will to reform. . . . Youmans [Spencer's chief American spokesman] in Henry George's presence denounced with great fervour the political corruption of New York and the selfishness of the rich in ignoring or promoting it when they found it profitable to do so. 'What do you propose to do about it?' George asked. Youmans replied 'Nothing! You and I can do nothing at all. It's all a matter of evolution. Perhaps in four or five thousand years evolution may have carried men beyond this state of things'.[2]

For one example from Europe, we can look at *Hitler's Table-Talk*:

If we did not respect the law of nature, imposing our will by the right of the stronger, a day would come when the wild animals would again devour us – then the insects would eat the wild animals, and finally nothing would exist except the microbes. . . . By means of the struggle the elites are continually renewed. The law of selection justifies this incessant struggle by allowing the survival of the fittest. Christianity is a rebellion against natural law, a protest against nature.[3]

Darwin himself set his face steadily against this kind of thing, which appalled him, and he went to considerable trouble in *The Descent of Man* to point out the deep general difference between the kind of qualities which could make it possible for a social group to survive over many generations,[4] and those that might keep a single individual afloat for his lifetime. Recent attempts to convict him too of 'Social Darwinism' do not refute this; they only show that (as is obvious) he was a man of his age; that there were limits to his criticisms of accepted ideas and institutions. This is true of all of us. But the particular mistake of treating all animal life as a matter of individual cut-throat competition was one which it was out of the question for Darwin to make, because he was a serious, full-time naturalist. He knew a great deal about the life of (for instance) birds, about parental care, warning cries and loyalty to the family and flock. 'The social instincts' were a central interest of his. In his mind they were always present in proper balance against the waste and cruelty of natural life.

Huxley and the exaggeration of conflict

T. H. Huxley, too, spoke out extremely strongly against the Spencerist mystique. Indeed he did so more often than Darwin, because in his day it had grown even more influential and was beginning to be an alarming force in politics. But Huxley's approach was significantly different just because he was not a naturalist. (His first ambition in life had been to be an engineer, and his one field trip on the *Rattlesnake* never really altered this angle.) To him, it was convincing enough that brutal competition ruled unchallenged over all other life-forms, provided that the human race was excepted. Human virtues, for Huxley, were a sudden 'ethical process' undertaken in reverse of the entire remainder of the 'cosmic process', that is, of laws governing everything else in the universe. This view leaves as quite legitimate a Hitlerian description of evolution, and only objects to the inclusion of man within it.

Huxley's attempt to stop at this point has been very widely imitated, but it is surely an almost impossible enterprise. If it had really been true that no organism stood in any relation to any other except a competitive one – if mutual destruction had been the only kind of interaction – the idea that a single species could suddenly engage on something else would indeed have been an extraordinary one. Alfred Russell Wallace's idea that an immortal soul had been suddenly implanted would be the least that would be needed to account for such a reversal, and even this seems quite inadequate for the job.[5] It is necessary to abandon this dramatic picture for something much more realistic. In fact, nature is green long before she is red, and must be green on a very large scale indeed to provide a context for redness. Organisms co-operate, profiting by each other's presence. As Darwin already pointed out in *The Origin of Species*, the 'struggle for existence' can often be described just as well as a mutual dependence.[6] And harmless coexistence as parts of the same ecosphere is also a very common relation. The astonishment with which Europeans tend still to see films of creatures of different kinds quietly grazing together, with carnivores resting placidly at no great distance, testifies to the unreality of our drama. This relation, too, is certainly more positive than the ignorant among us might suppose. A grazing animal which is kept in a field with another of a different species may not seem to pay it any attention, but if one is removed, the other will be much upset, and will pine. (It would be hard to say more of many coexisting pairs of human beings.) Among social creatures, positive gregariousness, a liking for each other's company, is the steady, unnoticed background for the conflicts. For less social creatures and for plants, the ability to live among others with a steady, mild exchange of benefits is usually a necessity. Ghiselin's story that all this co-operation is really only a carefully thought-out means to individual survival is just a gratuitous animistic fancy. It would be quite as sensible to say that the individuals are only there for the sake of the collectivity, which has subtly deluded them into supposing that they exist only for themselves.

Sociobiological sense and nonsense

The extraordinary thing about sociobiology is that, officially and properly speaking, it arises from the recognition of this sociality in advanced creatures and is simply a set of theories to account for it. Although its rhetoric treats that sociality as a myth, its theoretical task is to admit it as a fact and to make evolutionary sense of it. In essence, it is simply a study of the conditions under which social tendencies can be inherited in the process of natural selection. It arose from an insight of the great geneticist J. B. S. Haldane's about how capacities for altruistic behaviour could be passed on in evolution. If the Spencerist view of natural selection as plain, cut-throat, individual competition had been correct, this would simply have been impossible. Biologists had long realized this, but could not see what happened instead. What Haldane grasped was that tendencies leading to self-sacrifice *could* be transmitted provided that they were helpful to those who shared one's genes. This is 'kin-selection'. Willingness to die in defence of children or other relatives may destroy the first individual who has it, but if enough descendants who share that tendency are left, genes conducive to it survive and may possibly spread to the whole community. The question just is, how many descendants are enough? The story goes that Haldane, having thought of this in a pub, promptly seized an old envelope and became immersed in calculations. He finally emerged, declaring, 'I am willing to die for four uncles or eight cousins', that being the number who are needed to replace one's own genes in the tribal gene-pool. This is the sort of calculation which has been the prime business of sociobiologists ever since, and as Wilson puts it, the 'central theoretical problem' of the discipline is still 'how can altruism, which by definition reduces personal fitness, possibly evolve by natural selection?'[7] The calculations have now become very sophisticated, and often give surprising and interesting results. It is worth noticing, however, even in this initial casual story, how easily a confusion arises which has caused trouble ever since. Haldane spoke as if the answer to his genetic calculations could *decide* whether he would – or perhaps should? – die for his relatives. Of course all such strong, direct interpretations are wild and illicit. All that can reasonably be concluded from such evidence must remain very general and statistical, claiming merely that, where innate traits are transmitted without benefiting their owner, they must on average have benefited close kin in rough proportion to their closeness. The defence of children, in fact, does not stand alone. It is merely the strongest and simplest case.

15
Who or what is selfish?

Varieties of entities are not to be multiplied beyond necessity.
William of Occam

Hidden agents

Once this is realized, the puzzle about how altruistic traits can have developed ought to vanish; it has been solved. It continues, however, to worry sociobiologists and to present itself as somehow disturbing and anomalous. The 'problem of altruism' keeps recurring. To solve it, a model is developed whereby each organism is really aiming at its own advantage, but finds it not in this life but in 'inclusive fitness', that is in having many descendants. In some way this is held to remove the anomaly, to show that nothing was really done for the sake of others after all. Alternatively organisms themselves are seen as being genuinely altruistic, but being so only as the dupes of their genes, which appear as the real agents, egoists behind the scenes organizing the performance. Thus Richard Dawkins in *The Selfish Gene*:

> The argument of this book is that we, and all other animals, are machines created by our genes. Like successful Chicago gangsters, our genes have survived, in some cases for millions of years, in a highly competitive world. This entitles us to expect certain qualities in our genes. I shall argue that a predominant quality to be expected in a successful gene is ruthless selfishness. . . . If you wish . . . to build a society in which individuals co-operate generously towards a common good, you can expect little help from biological nature. Let us try to teach generosity and altruism, because we are born selfish.[1]

And E. O. Wilson:

> The individual organism is only the vehicle (of genes), part of an elaborate device to preserve and spread them with the least possible biochemical perturbation. . . . The organism is only DNA's way of making more DNA.[2]

Dawkins's remarks here show with beautiful clarity the full series of moves needed to complete this confusion. First, there is the old-fashioned 'beanbag' genetics, similar to that used by Monod, which supposed genes themselves to be isolated items tossed around in a randomizer, rather than the closely linked and regularly interworking components which they are now known to be. (Geneticists tend to despise sociobiology, and with some reason.) Then there is the animistic move – which Monod would have sharply rejected – of personifying the gene and describing this supposed competition in highly emotive terms as a deliberate project. Then comes the point where the quickness of the hand most needs to deceive the eye – the transfer of 'selfishness' from genes to organisms – '*we* are born selfish'. Finally there is the quite explicit drawing of a social moral – an extraordinary move if the behaviour of genes had really been the only thing under discussion – to the effect that human nature is totally iniquitous and unregenerate and any salvation for it can only come from some outside source. Since, in this highly anti-theistic context, no outside source is imaginable, this can only be the Huxleyan position in its most forbidding and discouraging form. It can only amount to a counsel of despair: the resigned, fatalistic acceptance of iniquity as inevitable which is the usual moral of Spencerist theorizing. This is strongly supported by Dawkins's habitual rhetoric in elevating the gene from its real position as a humble piece of goo within cells to a malign and all-powerful agent:

> It does not grow senile; it is no more likely to die when it is a million years old than when it is only a hundred. It leaps from body to body down the generations, manipulating body after body in its own way and for its own ends, abandoning a succession of mortal bodies before they sink in senility and death.
> The genes are the immortals.[3]

This impression, of course, depends on treating the type as a single entity and forgetting that each particular gene dies in the cell it belongs to. It would be no more and no less true to say that humanity did this, being represented successively by different individuals but transcending and outlasting them all. Again, the causal importance of genes is constantly exaggerated by a meaningless down-grading of other kinds of causes:

> By dictating the way survival machines and their nervous systems are built, genes exert ultimate power over behaviour. . . . Genes are the primary policy-makers; brains are the executives. . . . The logical conclusion to this trend (towards increasing intelligence) not yet reached in any species, would be for the genes to give the survival machine a single overall policy instruction – 'do whatever you think best to keep us alive'.[4]

If that were the situation, what could possibly be the sense of trying to defeat the genes by trying (for the first time in human history, as Dawkins explains) to start up some genuine altruistic behaviour – a move which must necessarily be just one more wily device on their part to secure their own survival? We should notice that 'ultimate power' is a meaningless phrase; science recognizes no causes which are not themselves subject to other causes, and the process of heredity has any number of other kinds of cause as well as genetic ones. But if there were indeed a being with 'ultimate power', it would presumably be one against which we were totally impotent. Though this idea has no place in science, it is extremely suggestive to the religious sensibilities. Worship, as we have already seen, is not only something carried out in Gothic buildings by people singing Hymns A. & M. It has many other forms and can be entirely informal. It is certainly the mood most strongly suggested by Dawkins's discussions of the gene.

The difficulty of not talking about motives

Sociobiological thinking, then, seems to conduct, side by side with its perfectly respectable attempt to account for the inherited co-operative tendencies of plants and animals, a very different and far less respectable myth-making activity. This commits it *either* (if individual selfishness is meant) to supporting a psychological egoism which is inconsistent with the very recognition that these tendencies exist, *or* (if gene-selfishness is preferred) to a story which is quite meaningless unless it is taken literally as a fatalistic acceptance of a non-human entity, endowed with such power over us that its purposes determine all our acts, and against which it is therefore senseless to strive. And if both ideas are combined, both drawbacks are available together.

Can this really be the situation? Officially, as has been pointed out, sociobiologists cannot be proposing psychological egoism, because they are not supposed to be talking about motives at all. But since they are claiming that what they call selfishness is indeed the root cause of most, if not all behaviour, what they say continually has this meaning. When readers understand it this way, the writers usually express surprise at such perverse misinterpretation of a harmless technical term. But they do it themselves all the time. In each sociobiological writer, an everyday Mr Hyde proceeds on his Hobbesian debunking psychoanalytic path, entirely regardless of scientific Dr Jekyll, who has just outlawed it. There is constant and explicit mention of motives, often even of conscious motives, as critics have repeatedly pointed out. Yet again, I give a few entirely typical examples. In *On Human Nature*, which appeared in 1978, after the matter had been well aired in controversy, Edward O. Wilson writes that nearly all altruism is of the 'soft-core' kind, which means that it is

ultimately selfish. The 'altruist' *expects* reciprocation from society for himself or his closest relatives. *His good behaviour is calculating, often in a wholly conscious way.* . . . The capacity for soft-core altruism can be expected to have evolved primarily by selection of individuals and to be deeply influenced by the vagaries of cultural evolution. *Its psychological vehicles are lying, pretense and deceit, including self-deceit, because the actor is most convincing who believes that his performance is real.* (my italics)[5]

This kind of story is continually stated, as it is here, explicitly as an account of motivation, an account which is meant to conflict with other possible accounts of it and prove them to be mistakes or lies. If these stories had really been only about evolutionary function, that clash could not arise.

As for the rare 'hard-core altruism' or genuine self-sacrifice, that, Wilson goes on to explain, is certainly no better. 'Pure, hard-core altruism based on kin-selection is the enemy of civilization.'[6] It is not (he explains) really an unusual case of genuine charity, but a mere mindless death-wish. That, again, makes it a motive, and Wilson's calling it 'irrational' can only mean that the only possible rational motive is self-interest. This can be nothing but crude, Hobbesian psychological egoism, altered only by the bizarre substitution of gene-maximization for self-preservation as the individual's aim.

Similar, as we have seen, is the message of M. T. Ghiselin:

The evolution of society fits the Darwinian paradigm in its most individualistic form. The economy of nature is competitive from beginning to end. Understand that economy, and how it works, and the underlying reasons for social phenomena are manifest. They are the means by which one organism gains some advantage to the detriment of another.

At this point, suddenly and without apology, the motives appear:

No hint of genuine charity ameliorates our vision of society, once sentimentalism has been laid aside. What passes for co-operation turns out to be a mixture of opportunism and exploitation. The impulses that lead one animal to sacrifice himself for another turn out to have their ultimate rationale in gaining advantage over a third; and acts 'for the good' of one society turn out to be performed for the detriment of the rest. Where it is in his own interest, every organism may reasonably be expected to aid his fellows. Where he has no alternative, he submits to the yoke of communal servitude. Yet given a full chance to act in his own interest, nothing but expediency will restrain him from brutalizing, from maiming, from murdering – his brother, his mate, his parent or his child. Scratch an 'altruist' and watch a 'hypocrite' bleed.[7]

That this sort of thing is pure fantasy, unrelated to any basis in science and indeed contrary to sociobiological findings so far as these do bear on motivation, has been mentioned already and will need to be mentioned again. We will come back to the whole background of mindless individualism which makes it seem plausible in the last two chapters. One thing, however, which deserves a moment's immediate attention is Ghiselin's use of inverted commas. It has evidently struck him that other terms besides 'altruism' may be affected by the strong solvent he wants to apply, and it is unlucky that he did not follow up this suspicion further. The hypocrisy involved in pretending to be altruistic would indeed be impossible in the world he invokes, and the scandalized, hysterical air of a hero unmasking villainy would be quite meaningless. Against a real Hobbesian background, one cannot play this melodrama at all.

David Barash, another central prophet of sociobiology, shows the same strange confusion, except that he is even more chronically prone to open psychologizing, using the idea of *unconscious* motivation in the hope of showing that this does not matter. That evolutionary promptings are unconscious selfish motives is a central theme of *Sociobiology; The Whisperings Within*[8] and their mode of working is conceived throughout in the way proclaimed by his opening manifesto: 'We will analyse parental behaviours, showing the underlying selfishness of our behaviour towards others, even our own children.' This is an impossible phrase. If 'selfishness' means here what sociobiologists say it means – a tendency to maximize one's own future gene-spread – it is directly displayed already in all care given by parents to children. There could be no further layer of it to reveal. If, by contrast, it names here something secret, underlying, and – as he suggests – disreputable, it must mean 'selfishness' as a motive, a we ordinarily understand that word. Nor are things any better in his book *Sociobiology and Behavior*:

> It is always nice to be nice to someone else. But it is unlikely to be adaptive. . . . Moral injunctions are simply irrelevant to the evolutionary process. Insofar as animals possess genetically mediated tendencies to behave for the benefit of another, the logic of evolution demands that these tendencies be grounded in underlying selfishness.[10]

Again, why *underlying*? The tendency to increase one's own gene-spread is not one motive lying hidden under another in the psychological layering, but a quite separate kind of causal property. All that is needed is to say that altruistic tendencies must be compatible with gene-promotion, that is they must not prevent it. And, as the central insight of sociobiology so usefully shows, behaviour that benefits others does not prevent it, provided that those others usually share one's genes. Kin-selection makes possible the spread of tendencies which are – considered as real motives – thoroughly unselfish in the ordinary sense, such as affection for one's children and the wish to help those in danger. It can make it extremely adaptive to be nice to others. And if we are worried about the primacy this gives to kin, we should notice that this is a very loose limitation. Because these tendencies do *not* spring from calculation, but from inherited disposition, they cannot be regularly switched off when someone less closely related heaves in sight. They are not strictly proportioned to blood relationship, but respond to many other cues, such as familiarity, admiration, liking and the special needs of others. And in human beings, the complexities of culture can give them a much wider range of channels than is possible for other species. In short, the Spencerist version of Hobbes, which supposed cut-throat individual competition to be the mechanism of evolution, is a howling error, as sociobiologists themselves have pointed out. But when we drop it, we have to drop also the sneering claim to peculiar worldly wisdom, the pride in seeing through all human pretensions to virtue, which have seemed to provide the luxury of superiority here. Virtue is as real a fact in the world as vice is, and the variety of genuine human motives is also real. They need to be studied on their own terms. Hobbes was only one contributor to the immensely complex, ancient and continuing business of investigating how motives work, and an exceptionally one-sided one. He cannot possibly be used to bypass it altogether.

The fatalist angle

Besides egoism, however, there seems to be in sociobiology something hostile to free will. It is often described as 'biological determinism'. This language, however, seems too wide. It is not clear that determinism – in the sense of belief in the regularity of nature – damages human freedom. If it does, we have got a real problem about the whole position of biology, quite independently of this controversy. The real blot on sociobiology is surely rather *fatalism*. There is a constant colourful invocation of non-human, but purposeful-sounding beings – usually the genes or DNA. These are treated as real calculating agents, manipulating human beings and other animals, who may suppose that they have purposes of their own, but are deceived in this, being in fact only ineffectual pawns, puppets or vehicles of these 'hidden masters'.[11] The tone is set in the opening manifesto of *Sociobiology* where Wilson, quoting with surprising approval that resolute vitalist Samuel Butler, proclaims that 'the organism is only DNA's way of making more DNA'.[12] What is the point of that *only*? What can it mean except that the motives and purposes which people think they have are *unreal*? They are being deceived and manipulated in the sort of way that someone is whose very desires have been instilled into him by others for their own purposes. Because evolutionary function is being treated as a motive, it is seen as a competitor with ordinary motives, and one with a deeper status, compared with which all these familiar motives are a mere superficial layer of humbug. This idea is displayed through a whole cornucopia of more or less mechanical metaphors, among which a favourite is that of programming computers. Thus Barash: '[Chess machines] are in the end nothing but the instructions that created them, and they can do no more than follow the ultimate design of their builders. Our builders are our genes.'[13]

An amazing variation on this is Wilson's metaphor of taking the dog for a walk: 'The genes hold culture on a leash. . . . Human behaviour . . . is the circuitous technique by which human genetic material has been and will be kept intact. Morality has no other demonstrable ultimate function.'[14] What sort of way is this to describe the relation between two interacting sets of partial causes? Would it be any less true to say that the climate holds genes on a leash? or that organisms do so? (Even culture, as sociobiologists concede, can have a marked effect on human gene-pools.) Officially this habit of personifying genetic causes as governors is meant to indicate that they are the only 'ultimate' causes. But the idea that any set of causes could be ultimate or one-way is, as we have mentioned, a most confused one, certainly not acceptable scientifically. What is actually conveys is the determination of sociobiologists to insist that their own causes are more important than those which are found by other methods of enquiry. The effect is, of course, to produce bad science. Environmental causes are neglected without any justification being given, and so are causes which flow from an individual itself during its lifetime (for instance, when a particular animal starts a migration or sets the example of tapping a new food-source). In human affairs, both these areas are of course of the first importance, since they cover the whole range of culture and individual action. To make it look plausible that sociobiology is as epoch-making as it claims, it is necessary to rule out the importance of these factors. It is also necessary to exaggerate the importance of genetic causes by ruling that no genetic variation can ever catch on except by being positively useful, that all is for the best in the best of all possible worlds. Unless this is so, it is not possible to reason back from the presence of a trait today and calculate the genetic factors which can have caused it to develop. The imposing neatness of the theory, then, demands that only genetic causes of behaviour should be taken seriously, and it is therefore presented in metaphors which rule out human freedom, presenting people, along with other animals and plants, as machines.

This attack on freedom is by no means a necessary consequence of admitting that there are these genetic causes at all. There certainly are, and their presence is harmless to freedom, indeed it is a precondition of it, since a mere piece of blank paper conditioned by its society would not be free. The enslaving element in sociobiology does not come from this, but from the refusal to admit other kinds of causes, a refusal which is often qualified or withdrawn at other places in these books, but returns in force whenever either the scientific argument or the rhetoric requires it. At that point the genetic forces appear as inescapable fates, and the rhetorical tone varies between reverence for their power and contempt for humans who suppose that any other element in life need concern them. It is strongly fatalistic, that is not just resigned to evils which have been proved inevitable, but more generally contemptuous of all human effort, from a sense of perceiving a conscious being which will not let it prevail. This fatalism, too, is linked to the egoism, since the being in question is treated as the prime case, the central example and source of the selfish motivation prevailing everywhere else. It is, in fact, a simple self-justifying projection of human selfishness.

The mystique of egoism and fatalism, then, is a real part of sociobiological writings. It cannot be shrugged off as a misinterpretation. And because of its stridency it is extremely influential. It has done, and is still doing, enormous harm. It has confirmed the

suspicions of social scientists and many others that there is something
endemically depraved and sinister about all discussion of human life
which uses a biological point of view and an evolutionary context. It is
useless for sociobiologists to plead what is perfectly true, that they are
not interested in exalting one race over another nor in proving
tendentious theories about the inheritance of intelligence. The continuity of their tone with that of earlier Spencerists who did do these
things is too strong. This is no accident either. The underlying moral
and psychological distortions really have not changed. The world-
picture which this rhetoric displays is still the one crudely projected
by those who glorified free-enterprise capitalism in its brash ex-
pansive stages by depicting both human nature and the biosphere as
framed in its image. It is used now, as it was then, to justify the
character faults typical of this cultural phase by treating them as
universal and inevitable.

   That image of living things as competitors is not of course a
complete fantasy. It has its place, if it is understood to be only one
image among many. But like all such images, when it is given
exclusive status and viewed as a direct description of the facts, it
grossly distorts thought. To give it this status, the actual behaviour
of plants and animals has to be carefully selected and often tendentiously described. The same handful of examples turns up again and
again, with the same swift extrapolation to the whole biosphere. And
much of the argument proceeds, quite independently of examples, by
computer simulation from imaginary cases. The dangers of this kind
of apriorism are in theory well known. Monod reasonably jeers at
Engels for explaining the growth of barley in terms of the Marxian
dialectic.[15] But any conceptual scheme followed confidently out of its
originally useful area, unchecked by criticism, is liable to lead to
similar absurdities. This is certainly happening in the study of animal
behaviour. One of its founding fathers, Niko Tinbergen, reissuing his
splendid book *The Study of Instinct* in 1969, commented with considerable alarm on the changes taking place there:

   We can apply to ethology what F. A. Beach once said of
   American psychology, that 'in its haste to step into the twen-
   tieth century' it had tried to rush through the preparatory,
   descriptive phase – a thing no natural science can afford to do.
   Having myself always spent long periods of exploratory watch-
   ing of natural events, of pondering about what exactly it was in
   the observed behaviour that I wanted to understand before
   developing an experimental attack, I find this tendency of
   prematurely plunging into quantification and experimentation,
   which I observe in many younger workers, really disturb-

ing. . . . A disproportionately great effort is channelled into questions of causation of behaviour. I feel very strongly that an equally intense effort ought to be made to understand the *effects* of behaviour. . . . It is tempting to ponder this over-emphasis on studies of causation. I believe that it is partly due to the fact that, as the development of physics and chemistry have shown, knowledge of the causes underlying natural events provides us with the power to manipulate these events and 'bully them into subservience'.[16]

In short, the deity being worshipped is power. As Tinbergen goes on to point out, this cannot any longer reasonably be viewed as a search for power for benevolent ends, in order to rescue the human race from its troubles. Our present troubles do not at all flow from a shortage of power but from a bad use of it. To prevent that bad use, we would need quite different kinds of enquiry, central among which is a better understanding of human motives. This is not to be looked for from a simple-minded discipline which starts by ruling that only one kind of motive is possible and occupies itself in trying to prove this – still less if it also maintains, at the same time, that it is not concerned with motives at all. Sociobiology is a false light because it is 'reductive' in the sense of ruling out other enquiries, of imposing its own chosen model as the only norm. But, far more serious than this negative drawback, it is also, like many such reductive disciplines, engaged on its own monstrous enterprise of illicit inflation. To balance the austere renunciation of religious ideas and of a normal view of human standing in the biosphere, which Wilson and Dawkins denounce, they offer us a mystique of power, vicarious indeed but evidently, from the fervent tone which celebrates it, none the less exciting for that.

16
Dreaming and waking

Like the choice between competing political institutions, that between competing paradigms proves to be a choice between incompatible modes of community life.

Thomas Kuhn

Dreams become nightmares

It is time to draw together the threads of this discussion. The myths and dramas we have been considering are various. They do not express a single system but a loose conglomerate of moods, attitudes and beliefs. What they have in common is, first, that they centre on the theme of evolution. Second, that while still using official scientific language about this theme, they are quite contrary to currently accepted scientific doctrines about it. Third, that they are powerfully emotive and sustaining. They are so shaped as to provide their adherents with a lively faith which can be an important element in the meaning of their lives.

Though they do not contain what for our culture are the central marks of a religion – belief in a personal deity and the explicit worship that goes with it – they seem to have grown up in response to needs which form some part of the group to which those giving rise to the religions belong. The tone in which they are expressed makes it impossible to dismiss them as mere accidental factual errors or formal survivals from obsolete doctrines. This tone is, typically, highly charged, though the charge varies strikingly over a range from the euphoric to the despairing.

At the euphoric end, a simple but groundless factual guarantee is offered of a secure and glorious future for the human race, a human heaven on earth as the inevitable end of the whole natural process. The mood is one of triumph tinged by reverence both for the future human beings themselves and for the force relied on to produce them, though it also contains elements of ordinary brash technological conceit. At the despairing end, a vision which is reminiscent of the darker elements in some traditional religions displays the universe not – as modern science officially requires – simply as a linked set of physical processes, but animistically, as a field for the play of malign forces attacking or exploiting humanity. Forms of this myth based on physics place this malign attitude in lifeless matter, centring on the mere failure of such matter to do something which could never rightly have been expected of it, namely to care for life. Forms based on population genetics place it either in the gene or in a mysterious, non-conscious analogue of motivation by 'selfishness', which is attributed to organisms themselves. Both pictures are fatalistic. Though nominally they tell us to fight back, they also emphasize human helplessness and thus a sense of being wholly dominated by whatever 'selfish' entities are described as active in the proceedings, whether personified genes or our own hidden motives.

The purely physical picture does not, of course, deal directly with evolution. It simply supplies a sinister, discouraging background for it, one which cannot fail to come into view if the observer's eye ever wanders past the margin of the euphoric vision. The genetic picture also does this on top of its more direct evolutionary meaning. Thus, both in Wilson and Dawkins, the apparently wholesome purpose of rebuking human pride by putting our species in its place in the grand evolutionary perspective, is reduced to absurdity by the exaltation of the gene as the entity which is to teach us our insignificance. Wilson and Dawkins preach that man is but dust, and is cut down as the flower of the field. But what is supposed to follow from this for our understanding of life is an arbitrary, selective debunking of all non-egoistic motivation. In their gloomier moments, these writers, along with Monod and Weinberg, seem to resemble chiefly those pagan poets of the Dark Ages whose disgust and contempt for the world led them (as has been remarked) to imitate pretty well everything in Christianity except faith, hope and charity.

The unavoidability of meaning

Why does this happen? There is something of a dilemma here for dramatizers. On the one hand, the physical picture in its literal, impersonal form is scarcely graspable at all by the human imagination. We can repeat figures and formulae which are supposed to describe vast cosmological processes, but they mean very little to us.

And there certainly seems no reason why they should have any consequences for our present actions or feelings. In themselves they are meaningless for us. But a hunger for meaning is central to our lives. It is not just an accidental, irrelevant emotion, needing to be brushed aside as an interference with thought. It is the wider motive of which our theoretical curiosity is only a part. It is the impulse of our imaginations to order the world with a view to understanding and contemplating it — something which must be done before theory-building can ever start. To keep this wider impulse out of factual investigations is not just emotionally difficult, it is conceptually impossible. Yet to let it in is to relate science to our most general responses to life, responses which normally involve drama and very easily build up into some kind of religious attitude.

Does the quest for meaning have to have this outcome? Many great scientists, such as Einstein, have found it an entirely natural one. It might seem as if smaller scientists, with smaller ideas, could avoid it more easily. And it is of course a misfortune of our highly-organized age that quite a lot of people do now become professional enquirers simply for social reasons, without ever having felt strong theoretical curiosity at all. For them science is small. It can never be anything but 'normal science', a rather dull, pre-regulated occupation detached from the central meaning of their lives. But since boredom, which is the natural response to such unmeaning occupations, is painful, it is no wonder that they snatch at such myths and dramas as are made available to them, and readily accept even ones which, like those we have mentioned, are quite illicit scientifically. The kind of imper-sonality which science requires simply cannot extend to total absence of meaning. It cannot demand — as is sometimes suggested — that all facts should be treated as equally important. Facts have to be connected up somehow, and in every system of connection some are more important than others. Enquiry cannot remain atomistic, stack-ing them separately in standard boxes; it imposes priorities. And the systematized findings cannot remain colourless, detached from the general purposes of life. The kind of importance they have, the kind of colouring they take on, will be determined by the general world-picture which the enquirer accepts.

The choice is not between integrating facts into one's world-picture and keeping them detached from it. It is between good and bad world-pictures. The impersonality required is not total detachment, because this is impossible. It is responsible objectivity — the far more difficult task of becoming more aware of one's world-picture, doing all one can to correct its more obvious faults, and showing it as plainly as possible to one's readers in order that they may know fully what they are accepting. As far as emotional tone goes, this calls for what

Darwin offered: the very careful avoidance of all cheap and simple ranting which might carry people away to accept one's views wholesale, but also the full, scrupulous expression of attitudes and feelings which seem to one, after thought, to be called for by the subject-matter. This is not unlike the kind of impersonality needed for good art, a transcending of one's personal limitations to reach attitudes valuable to everybody.

Science is not just a natural phenomenon; it is something done by people. Since people are essentially purposive beings, it cannot fail to reflect their general conceptions of what constitutes an important purpose. We can see this extremely clearly when we look at cases at some distance. It is plain to us now how seventeenth-century thought, dominated by the two linked ideas of God and Mechanism, achieved its remarkable results by treating the universe as a huge, changeless, eternal, divinely manufactured clock. We can also see – not directly but because of later developments – how that model had its limitations and eventually needed to be altered. We see too how nineteenth-century thought, fired with the idea of individualistic progress by the Industrial Revolution, by expanding empire and by the social-contract model, accepted a quite different, dynamic picture of a steadily evolving world, a world in which enlightened self-interest was a sufficient force to lead life all the way from the primal soup to a predictable earthly heaven. We can by now see the historical reasons why such a picture should ever have been projected on to the cosmos, and also a great many reasons why it too, in spite of the good work which it has made possible, was bound in the end to prove inadequate. Some of its earliest and most obviously crude forms have long been denounced under the inappropriate name of 'Social Darwinism'. But in its general outline it still persists, because to get rid of such a picture one has to replace it fully by another, and this has not yet been done. There are probably dozens of different elements in our thought which still need radical changes before we can free ourselves from the distorting influences of this picture, even though we well know that there is a great deal wrong with it, and have long been accustomed to use the word 'Victorian' patronizingly, as a term of abuse.

Demons and their dangers

In this book, I am trying to deal with a few of them; most deeply, perhaps, with the idea that what was chiefly needed for the current phase of this splendid progress was just to get rid of religion and replace it by science. The distortion that afflicts science when it is put into the place of religion is a central part of my theme. And it does not seem to me to be altogether an accident that attempts to remove religion produced a vacuum into which science was to some extent sucked. In looking at the way people have expressed themselves in the course of these attempts, I am struck by the strong intellectual need there is to have some view of the cosmos as a whole. It does seem to me that the project of entirely depersonalizing this view may not be a possible one. Possibly, for human beings, the only alternative to thinking of the universe as, in some vast and remote way, purposive and benign, is to think of it as purposive and radically malignant. It may simply not be within our capacity – except of course by just avoiding thought – to think of it as having no sort of purpose or direction whatever. And since the notion that it is radically malignant is a crazy one, benignity seems to be the only usable option.

This sense of cosmic benignity can of course remain extremely remote and, by ordinary standards, impersonal. It is not the same thing as belief in a distinct creator, still less in a personal God who can be addressed. Of course the boundaries of these concepts are not easy to fix, and language is hard to use effectively in discussing them. But it does seem clear that people who firmly deny this benignity are extremely easily led on to assert that something actually vicious is present instead. They very readily begin to talk like A. E. Housman about 'whatever brute or blackguard made the world', or say like Hardy that 'the President of the Immortals had finished his sport with Tess'. Obviously this kind of talk has its passing value as a corrective to a complacent or childish kind of religion. But if it is taken seriously as more than a passing corrective, it seems at once to become no less superstitious than what it was trying to correct, and also far less usable for life.

Such visions cannot be inert. They exist to guide conduct; it is of their nature to influence life. But the only practical consequences which this one seems capable of producing are abominable. It imposes either a fatalistic, paralysing resignation to human helplessness before destructive forces, or a positive justification for joining them in selfish mayhem. Also, like the Newtonian picture, this Spencerian one makes it very hard to criticize the basic political pattern of the age. As the earlier one protected monarchical government, the later one protects competitive individualism. Each reflects that currently accepted pattern as part of the eternal order of things, invoking our respect for science to make it look unchangeable. The modern one rules that only one form of human activity can escape this general paralysis, namely the practice of science itself. The reasons for this exception are not at all clear. Undoubtedly, however, it has played a great part in getting the myth accepted. Without it, the moral bankruptcy of these ideas would have been obvious at once, and the faults of the whole underlying conceptual scheme would have been much more quickly seen.

Daylight

As it is, they do seem to be beginning to be seen today. Although euphoric visions of a guaranteed human future still persist – although the word 'future' itself is still often used as the name for a simple, endless technological heaven – most people who think at all are now aware that objective probability unfortunately does not today offer us anything of the kind. Even among the rosy predictions still being given, we increasingly often hear the quite different message that this or that technical fix must be tried *because* things are getting very bad, and desperate measures are called for. Apocalyptic prophecies alternate with the complacent ones in an uncontrolled way – a confusing situation which is the price paid for our long refusal to understand how much the complacent ones were worth. There is little to be said for refusing to wake up, even on a cold morning, if the dreams which we would like to prolong are themselves increasingly invaded by spasms of nightmare.

It cannot really be plausible today that world hunger, destruction of the biosphere and the arms race merely form a slight temporary difficulty which our civilization cannot fail to surmount as it lifts us onward in the steady, inevitable progress of humanity. Naturally there is now an enormous demand for theorists who will reassure us by saying that there is no serious threat here. To their credit, physical scientists have in general refused to deliver any such shoddy article. Ecologists, geographers, biologists, oceanographers, agriculturalists, nutrition experts and the rest have mainly confirmed what the anthropologists and modern historians were also saying, that things are bad and rapidly getting worse. The only speciality that still finds itself in a position to make reassuring noises is economics, a fact which may have something to do with its habitual practice of never looking very far ahead. Even if the economists were right in their own field, however, the enlightened behaviour of men in markets would scarcely be enough to save the world. It could not cancel all the other messages, which read, not that nothing can be done, but that a great deal of what is far from customary needs to be done, and done quickly. On this consensus, so deep are the current dangers that there is no serious possibility at all of predicting the long-term future of mankind. Unimaginable though we may find it, our civilization might well collapse, and there is a real possibility that the species might become extinct. Nuclear winter is not just a pacifist dream; it is a fully supported scientific prediction of what should be expected if even a tithe of existing nuclear weapons were ever used.[1] It could be the end not only of mankind but of most other advanced terrestrial life as well. These things sound as mythical as the visions we have been considering, but they are sober scientific prose, produced quite contrary to the myths of the age, not arising out of them..So are the predictions about the extinctions which are likely to take place even if war is avoided, simply from human expansion and destruction of habitat. So are the predictions of world famine, some of which (relating to Ethiopia) the governments of the world have, as I write, just been neglecting and have been surprised to find verified.

Science, which raised the curtain on dazzling visions of the human future and for some time sustained them, now comes forward to bring down that curtain. I find it admirably symbolic that Carl Sagan, a great prophet of space travel, is now taking the foremost place in spreading the news about nuclear winter. To my mind, that looks like a notable process of maturing, a formidable journey from dreams to reality. This is not to deny, of course, that humankind, if it pulls itself together to meet its current challenge, might return to many of the ambitious projects which it has today, and might even consider manned space expeditions worth making. But at present what is needed above all is attention to the current dangers. It is in that sense only that we can have any business now to occupy ourselves with the concept of 'the future'.

17
The limits of individualism

There is also I know not what of fashion on this side; and by
some means or other, the whole world almost is run into the
extremes of insensibility towards the distresses of their fellow-
creatures; so that general rules and exhortations must always be
on the other side.

Bishop Butler

In the lonely crowd

How are we to adjust to this new situation, a situation made so much
harder for us by the exceptionally euphoric myths on which we grew
up? Certainly mankind cannot bear very much reality. Confronting
here the father and mother of all problems, we may deceive ourselves
in two ways. We may try to pretend that the problem is smaller than it
is, that things have not yet gone badly wrong. This will not get us far.
More often we take refuge in fatalism, in concluding that there is
nothing that we can do. Obviously, however, there is one part of the
problem which is more under our control than the rest. This is our
own way of thinking, the general ethos of the west. That does seem to
have certain things dangerously wrong with it. Many people, therefore, call for a new ethic. What ought we to do about this?

John Passmore, in his thorough philosophical discussion, has very
properly pointed out that new ethics cannot be bought like new hats.[1]
Ethics, being patterns of incredible complexity, have to be evolved,
not manufactured, and they always build on what went before. Like
paradigms, they are part of the world-picture. And old ethics do not
go in the dustbin. The range of moral insights possible to the human
race probably does not change much, and all of them go on being

needed on occasion. What does change drastically is the emphasis. Quite a small change in emphasis can make an enormous difference to life. In every age, morality has a bias. It is obvious to those who come after, but history shows us how hard even the most astute people find it to detect where the bias of their own age lies. As the Devil points out in *The Screwtape Letters*, the results can be highly ludicrous:

> The game is to have them all running about with fire extinguishers when there is a flood, and all crowding to that side of the boat which is already gunwale under. Thus (says the Devil) we make it fashionable to expose the dangers of enthusiasm at the very moment when they are all becoming worldly and lukewarm. . . . Cruel ages are put on their guard against Sentimentality, feckless and idle ones against Respectability, lecherous ones against Puritanism, and whenever all men are really hastening to be slaves or tyrants, we make Liberalism the prime bogey.[2]

What bias, then, is now misleading us? I am suggesting that it is an unbridled, exaggerated individualism, taken for granted as much by the left as by the right – an unrealistic acceptance of competitiveness as central to human nature. People not only *are* selfish and greedy, they hold psychological and philosophical theories which tell them they *ought* to be selfish and greedy. And the defects of those theories have not been fully noticed.

In a sense which we have just been exploring, Social Darwinism or Spencerism is the unofficial religion of the west. The official western religion, Christianity, is well known to be rather demanding and to have its eye on the next world rather than this one. In such situations, other doctrines step in to fill the gap. People want a religion for this world as well. They find it in the worship of individual success. The fast buck itself is not exactly an end, since nobody can eat paper, but it is valued primarily both as a means to this success and as a sign of it.

Contemporary greed is sometimes called *materialism*. This does not seem to quite right, since people's material needs are limited, and could all be met at quite modest expense. Most of the goods greedily demanded are wanted for other reasons which are imaginative and symbolic. They are seen as necessary assurances of individual status within the boiling maelstrom of contemporary western life, a setting where crowding and constant movement impose social strains unknown to almost any other culture. And it is widely believed that the theory of evolution proves this kind of narrowly self-assertive motivation to be not just an unfortunate response to certain local social conditions, but fundamental, universal and in some sense the law of life. Mystical reverence for such deities as progress, nature and the life-force is then invoked to explain and justify cut-throat competition.

As we have seen, such a view of the natural motivation of our species is simply a mistake, a projection of current interests. It finds no support in biology. I have not attacked Spencerism in the usual way, namely, for reasoning illicitly from facts to values. That attack would concede its view of the facts as correct, which it is not. I have pointed out instead how badly it is wrong on its facts, and how much we need to get these very important facts right.

Not all facts are irrelevant to values, only some. This particular set of facts about natural motivation seems relevant enough. *If there were* a social species so extraordinary as to be by its nature entirely egoistic, it would have little choice but to live egoistically, in unmitigated competition, conducting a war of all against all, or controlling it only by bargains made for safety. But it is hard to see how such a creature could ever have become social or capable of reasoning, which requires attention to the views of others. Certainly it could never have entertained – as we are now doing – any criticism of egoism. There is overwhelming evidence that ours is not such a species.

The bias of social contract ethics

Why, in that case, should anybody ever have thought that it was? Here we reach the sore place, the nub of the problem. Individualism is tied up with much that we rightly value very highly. Ever since the Renaissance, it has been a key project of our culture to free individuals from the pressure of their social background and to enable them to stand alone. Endless devoted efforts have been made to pry each loose from his family, his state, his church and any other shell to which he might cling, and allow him – indeed force him – to think and act for himself. (Himself, but not always herself – a feature which for some time made the project look more promising than it actually was. Altruism was still expected of women.) The project was far wilder and more ambitious than was usually noticed.

Liberal political theory, from Hobbes onward, called on each citizen to view himself as primarily a distinct, autonomous atom, unlinked to his fellow atoms unless he contracts to join them. The sources of this project, indeed, are far older; it started with the Greeks. Their efforts to encourage individual thought and responsibility gave rise to all that is most distinctive in our civilization. Christianity, with its emphasis on the separate, irreplaceable value of each human soul, also played a key part in the drama, which came into full flower in the Enlightenment. The careful separating out of each soul from its social background has of course been responsible for an immense amount that is distinctive and valuable in the achievements of our civilization. No other culture has carried it nearly so far. No wonder that to many people it never looked, until lately, as if we could ever have too much of that good thing, individualism.

What has happened now, however, is that we seem to be left with little conceptual ground to stand on when we want to make the opposite kind of point and declare that the world is, after all, in some ways actually one, and that human beings exist only as parts of it. Why, for instance, should a Brazilian farmer *not* cut down the rain forest to raise beef for a few years, moving on when the soil is exhausted and abandoning it to become a desert? or why should the local manager for a multinational company not do the same? Are these people not free agents? Contract-based prudential objections can certainly be found. We can say that the forest is a reservoir of species which may prove invaluable for medicine and other technologies, that the Indians (if provoked too far) will attempt reprisals, and that the effect of forest clearance will probably endanger everyone in the long run, since it would impoverish the whole of Brazil. To this, however, he may simply and consistently reply that, whatever happens, rich Brazilians will always be safer than poor Brazilians, and multinational companies making quick profits will always be safer than those making slow ones. The point of the present schemes is exactly to increase riches and thereby individual safety.

Now, it may be thought that these people have failed to grasp the full meaning of the social contract. And it is true that contractual ethics usually is not expressed in this crude, predatory, ding-dong form. As philosophers display it, it can incorporate all sorts of impersonal, rational safeguards, hypothetical role-exchanges, veils of ignorance, and similar public-spirited devices. But if the atomic individuals who do the original contracting really conceive of themselves as essentially separate, it is hard to see why they should ever bother about these procedures. The point is not just that, since they are wicked, they are unlikely to consider others, but that, since they are separate, they can have no reason to do so. They might happen to fancy such thoughts, but there is nothing in their motivation to make them relevant.

Of course, there are further appeals to prudence which can be made. Calculations based on the hope of becoming immensely rich are rather unreliable. A more realistic, enlightened, Hobbesian self-interest might tell them to be less destructive, merely as an insurance policy. But narrowly selfish people tend not to be very imaginative, and often fail to look far ahead. That is one thing which the Industrial Revolution so far has made clear to us, and there is good reason for it. Exclusive self-interest tends by its very nature *not* to be enlightened, because the imagination which has shrunk so far as to exclude consideration for one's neighbours also becomes weakened in its power to foresee future changes. Vice has its martyrs, as well as virtue. A great many aspiring egoists have crashed in attempting the feat which Howard Hughes, in his way, brought off, and his success – such as it was – no doubt involved luck as well as cleverness.

The psychology of this is very important. Hobbes really was mistaken in supposing that people could defer satisfaction indefinitely from prudence, that they were sufficiently patient, dispassionate, timid and far-sighted to build a harmonious world purely on bargains for self-interest. When other, more direct social motives are weakened, as they are today, human prudence alone turns out quite unequal to the job. On every side now we can see people busily engaged in sawing off the branches on which they (along with many others) are sitting, intent only on getting those branches to market before the price of timber falls. Prudence does not prevent this destruction. It is therefore clear that what did to some extent prevent it in the past was a set of motives quite distinct from prudence and owing nothing to contract. They are, of course, the motives which until recently inhibited the free development of technology. They are motives like conventionality, identification with one's group, the fear of *hubris*, of novelty and excess, loyalty, respect for one's elders, and a general awe at the mysterious otherness of nature.

It would seem a good idea that we should now overhaul this mixed bag of motives carefully, examine them, and sort out what is useful in them from what is not, re-expressing the useful part in terms suitable to our own day. There is plenty of material for this. Anthropologists, showing us how the cumulative nature of culture demands continuity and how the murder of a culture can kill its members, have given us reason to have a far better opinion of conventionality, loyalty, identification with the group, and respect for the elders than we used to. Ecologists have pointed out that on the physical side there was good reason for the fear of *hubris*, and for awe at the mysterious otherness of nature. They make clear that we have only the most superficial understanding of the vast physical systems on which we depend, so that awe – as well as caution in change – is entirely rational. Social psychologists have drawn attention to the complex dependence of human individuals on their background. Ethologists have shown from animal parallels how deep the function of this is likely to be. In psychoanalysis, transactional thinking has broken the grip of Freudian egoism and made it possible to acknowledge human otherness.

In general, whatever reservations anyone may have about particular parts of this development, it must emerge that a whole set of communal aspects of life, which used to be despised and attributed to the corrupting influence of religion, now appear as both necessary and understandable in terms of the sciences. They are not just instruments of political oppression but essential conditions of life.

The dark side of the Enlightenment

There remains, however, a general difficulty, inhibiting us as western intellectuals from even considering these motives. Our superegos are very unwilling to allow it. Internalized in each of us is a voice which speaks with the accents of Voltaire and Rousseau, of Mill, Hume, Tom Paine and Mary Wollstonecraft: a voice which says, 'Was it for this that we defied the priests, the fathers, and the kings? Can anything be more important than individual liberty?'

Unluckily, this voice comes now like a fire extinguisher in a flood. It can distract us, but not help us. Of course, there are still tyrants. But what chiefly confronts us today is not an Easter Island row of ossified traditional patriarchs, but a chaotic mob of dollar-snatching cormorants, doing damage of an order undreamed of in previous ages. Even in private life, it seems possible that sheer confusion of conflicting claims now makes at least as much misery – if not more – as the confident appeal to traditional authority. But the public issue is the one before us now. Observing the cormorants, we are in no doubt that we ought to disapprove of them, but our disapproval is forced to be indirect. Our tradition now lacks the natural, obvious concepts by which most of the human race would denounce unbridled human predation. We cannot say – as almost any other culture could – that these people are betraying their ancestors, offending the ghosts, that they are sacrilegious outcasts and matricides, destroying the land which gave them birth. Very likely we are right to throw away this language, but we should not throw away with it the power of expressing certain evident and crucial truths.

Of course, human beings are distinct individuals. But they are also tiny, integral parts of this planet – framed by it, owing everything to it, and adapted to a certain place among its creatures. Each can indeed change its life, but does not originally invent it. Each receives life in a family (as a petal does in a flower), in a country (as the flower does on the tree), and in the biosphere (as the tree does in the forest). Our environment gives us nearly everything we have and if, even as adults, we were deposited with all alien modern conveniences on a planet of Sirius, we would (with all due respect to Carl Sagan) be no more than shrivelled petals.

All this is no derogation of our essential dignity, because dignity is meaningless without a context. The only person who might conceivably exist and make sense on his own is God, and even He apparently prefers not to try it, since He creates the world. And whatever might be true of God, man is no god, but a social being and a part of the fauna of this planet. When the architects of our present ethics were campaigning for individual liberty, this did not need saying. It could safely be taken for granted. Today, with the damage which unrealistic individualism is doing both to the physical life of the planet and to the personal happiness of individuals, it does need saying.

We do not exactly need new concepts, since suitable ones do exist in our culture. (John Passmore is right to insist that such concepts should always be looked for and used when possible, because the idea of an entirely unprecedented moral insight occurring for the first time in this epoch is a fishy one, and people are quite properly suspicious of it.) The concepts exist. But both they and our current moral ideas need adapting in order to show their reality and importance. Our world-picture needs to be changed, and is indeed already beginning to be changed, to give them much greater prominence. What is now, rather oddly, beginning to be known as 'libertarianism' – the Nozick-ian, explicit defence of the competitive ideal as primary against all others – is a reaction against this incipient changing. Social, co-operative ideals have to be seen as taking a major, rather than a minor, part in practical argument. Moral changes are perhaps, above all, changes in what kind of thing people are ashamed of. Till lately, our age was accustomed to classing environmental considerations as marginal, and so treating any emphasis on them as sentimental, emotional, unrealistic and – above all – insufficiently virile. (Some influential libertarians, notably Rousseau and Nietzsche, have been obsessed with virility, a notion which still confuses radical thought.)

The excesses of commercial free enterprise may be repulsive to us, but we are still committed to seeing it as in some way proper and admirable, because it is still a form of freedom. It appears as a monstrous parody of our most sacred ideals. If there is really nothing more important than freedom, must that parody at some level be embraced and accepted? Is there no way to be sure that the destroyer is not an admirable Nietzschean superman?

Using our heads

When things look as bad as this, it is usually best to ask: need we have started from here? Having begun to consult the eighteenth-century oracle, perhaps it will help to carry the process further. What has the Enlightenment really got to tell us? It is pleasant to imagine the expression which would rise on the faces of Voltaire, Rousseau and Kant, if (having recalled them, much against their principles, from the tomb) we explain to them that we find ourselves – two centuries after their deaths – so imprisoned conceptually by their discoveries that we are unable to tackle the problem of adapting them to a new emergency and a different age. They themselves were bold innovators. In so far as anybody has ever produced a new ethic, they did. They knew that when the state of the world changes, new ideas must be used. What the ghost of Voltaire requires is that we should be willing to twist the tails of *all* sacred cows, including those from his own herd. The ghost of Rousseau tells us, first and foremost, to understand our own nature and its place in the nature of the universe. As for Kant, he advises us above all to think independently and freely. And Nietzsche would have had as low an opinion of the multinationals as he had of the nationalists and anti-Semites of his day. None of them provides any ready-made conclusions, nor guarantees that the emphasis we need will be the same that was called for in their day. All changes of emphasis in morality are correctives, answering temporary needs. No such change can be final.

Right through the seventeenth and eighteenth centuries, it was reasonable for enquiring people to see their main enemy as feudalism, the theocratic and monarchical hierarchy in which individuals were paralysingly embedded. The Industrial Revolution, releasing them to become socially mobile, naturally appeared on the whole as a liberating force. This background explains why Darwin's views, when they appeared, were put to such extraordinary use. The existing intellectual furniture produced a powerful optical illusion, making the doctrine of the survival of the fittest look like the precept 'each for himself and the devil take the hindmost'. Evolution seemed to endorse egoism and, thereby, unbridled capitalism.

Despite protests from both scientists and philosophers, people still find this interpretation almost irresistible. It accounts for two rather serious confusions today. The first and cruder one is the recent revival of creationism among educated people and even among some scientists. The project of treating the time scale of the Genesis story literally, as a piece of history, is an amazing one, which serious biblical scholars at least as far back as Origen (AD 200) have seen to be unworkable and unnecessary. The reason why people turn to it now seems to be that the only obvious alternative story – evolution – has become linked with a view of human psychology which they rightly think both false and immoral. The second, rather subtler, confusion is what generates the tangle of myths and dramas we have been considering in this book – a tangle of which sociobiology, the element so far most noticed, is only a part. In these myths, Spencerism emerges as a whole, containing many seductive elements which have made the crude, depressing, unconvincing psychology seem accept-

ole. The confident vision of future glory, and of a destiny central to
ιe cosmos, is a sweetener which makes everything else easy to
vallow. This use of a dazzling future to distract believers from the
resent, thus excusing immediate crimes and confusions, is some-
ιing Spencerism shares with many forms of Marxism, Nietzscheism
ιd Christianity. Among these, Spencerism differs in having had for a
me the advantage of actually producing instalments on its heaven in
ιe form of aeroplanes, guns and TV sets. Good arguments, however,
·e something it is still uncommonly short of, and the trouble with a
ιyth of progress is that its existing successes always lead to a demand
·r more. The gap between promise and performance is widening;
ιgnitive dissonance is beginning to set in. I think this is a very serious
ement in the malaise of the present day. It is extremely urgent to try
ιd adapt our thoughts realistically to a world which has no fixed
ιneral direction either upward or downward, but which is likely to
ιry largely according to what we do.

When the light of criticism is turned on these current myths, it may
erhaps emerge that there is less difference between the two kinds of
ιnfusion just mentioned than at first appears. Both creationism and
pencerism seem radically to confuse the functions of religion and
:ience, attempting to produce an amalgam which will do the work of
ιth. In doing so, both seem to distort not just the province which
ιey are trying to take over, but also the one in whose name they want
ι make the conquest. Much more attention is needed to the meaning
· these abstractions. And it ought to emerge as part of the wider
:thinking through which we have to forge ourselves a new world-
icture.

This cannot be done quickly. It needs long and careful work to get
s clear about the mistakes which our present picture incorporates
ithout throwing away those parts of the truth which it does convey.
think it is best to end this book by making some attempt to
ut individualism into perspective. This seems to be the element in
ιr currently accepted morality which does most to make the
ιuasi-scientific myths we have been discussing look plausible. Its
mitations go a long way both to support egoism and to make us feel
ιstified, as humans, in neglecting the rest of the biosphere. It has
lso, in its hypertrophied form, generated the crazy concepts of
eedom which power the visions of Monod and Richard Dawkins.
ccordingly, the philosophy on which it rests had better be consi-
ered in our last chapter.

18
The vulnerable world and its claims on us

Is meanness always rational?

Had Robinson Crusoe any duties on his island?

When I was a philosophy student, this used to be a familiar conundrum, which was supposed to pose a very simple question: namely, can you have duties to yourself? Mill, they correctly told us, said no. 'The term duty to oneself, when it means anything more than prudence, means self-respect or self-development and for none of these is anyone accountable to his fellow-creatures.'[1] Kant, on the other hand, said yes. 'Duties to ourselves are of primary importance and should have pride of place . . . nothing can be expected of a man who dishonours his own person.'[2]

There is a serious disagreement here, not to be sneezed away just by saying 'it depends on what you mean by duty.' Much bigger issues are involved. But quite how big has, I think, not yet been fully realized. To grasp this, I suggest that we rewrite a part of Crusoe's story, so as to bring in sight a different range of concerns, thus:

Sept. 19, 1685. This day I set aside to devastate my island. My pinnace being now ready on the shore, and all things prepared for my departure, Friday's people also expecting me, and the wind blowing fresh away from my little harbour. I had in mind to see how all would burn. So then, setting sparks and powder craftily among certain dry spinneys which I had chosen, I soon had it ablaze, nor was there left, by the next dawn, any green stick among the ruins.

Now, work on the style how you will, you cannot make that into convincing paragraph. Crusoe was not the most scrupulous of men but he would have felt an invincible objection to this senseless destruction. So would the rest of us. Yet the language of our moral tradition has tended strongly, ever since the Enlightenment, to make that objection unstateable. All the terms which express that a claim is serious or binding – duty, right, law, morality, obligation, justice – have been deliberately narrowed in their use so as to apply only within the framework of contract, to describe only relations holding between free and rational agents. Since it has been decided *a priori* that rationality has no degrees and that cetaceans are not rational, it follows that, unless you take either religion or science fiction seriously, we can only have duties to humans, and sane, adult, fully responsible humans at that.

Now the morality we live by certainly does not accept this restriction. In common life we recognize many other duties as serious and binding, though of course not necessarily overriding. If philosophers want to call these something else instead of 'duties', they must justify their move. We have here one of these clashes between the language of common morality (which is of course always to some extent confused and inarticulate) and an intellectual scheme which arose in the first place from a part of that morality, but has now taken off on its own and claims authority to correct other parts of its source.

There are always real difficulties here. As ordinary citizens we have to guard against dismissing such intellectual schemes too casually; we have to do justice to the point of them. But as philosophers, we have to resist the opposite temptation of taking the intellectual scheme as decisive, just because it is elegant and satisfying, or because the moral insight which is its starting-point is specially familiar to us. Today, this intellectualist bias is often expressed by calling the insights of common morality mere 'intuitions'. This is quite misleading, since it gives the impression that they have been reached without thought, and that there is, by contrast, a scientific solution somewhere else to which they ought to bow as there might be if we were contrasting commonsense 'intuitions' about the physical world with physics or astronomy. Even when they do not use that word, however, philosophers often manage to give the impression that whenever our moral views clash with any simple, convenient scheme, it is our *duty* to abandon them. Thus the philosopher G. R. Grice:

> It is an inescapable consequences of the thesis presented in these pages that certain classes cannot have natural rights: animals, the human embryo, future generations, lunatics and children under the age of, say, ten. In the case of young children at least, my experience is that this consequence is found hard to accept. But it is a consequence of the theory; it is, I believe, true; and I think we should be willing to accept it. At first sight it

seems a harsh conclusion, but it is not nearly so harsh as it appears.[3]

But it is in fact extremely harsh, since what he is saying is that the treatment of children ought not to be determined by their interests, but by the interests of the surrounding adults capable of contract, which of course can easily conflict with them.

In our own society, he explains, this does not actually make much difference, because parents here are so benevolent that they positively want to benefit their children; and accordingly here 'the interests of children are reflected in the interests of the parents.' But this, he adds, is just a contingent fact about us. 'It is easy to imagine a society where this is not so', where, that is, parents are entirely exploitative. 'In this circumstance, the morally correct treatment of children would no doubt be harsher than it is in our society. But the conclusion has to be accepted.' Grice demands that we withdraw our objections to harshness, in deference to theoretical consistency. But 'harsh' here does not mean just 'brisk and bracing' like cold baths and a plain diet. (There might well be more of those where parents do feel bound to consider their children's interests.) It means unjust.

Our objection to unbridled parental selfishness is not a mere matter of tone or taste; it is a moral one. It therefore requires a moral answer, an explanation of the contrary value which the contrary theory expresses. Grice and those who argue like him take the ascetic, disapproving tone of people who have already displayed such a value, and who are met by a slovenly reluctance to rise to it. But they have not displayed that value. The ascetic tone cannot be justified merely by an appeal to consistency. An ethical theory which, when consistently followed through, has iniquitous consequences is a bad theory and must be changed. Certainly we can ask whether these consequences really are iniquitous; but this question must be handled seriously. We cannot directly conclude that the consequences cease to stink the moment they are seen to follow from our theory.

Sociality and social contracts

The theoretical model which has spread blight in this area is, of course, that of social contract, to fit which the whole cluster of essential moral terms which I mentioned – right, duty, justice and the rest – has been progressively narrowed. This model shows human society as a spread of standard social atoms, originally distinct and independent, each of which combines with others only at its own choice and in its own private interest. This model is drawn from physics, and from seventeenth century physics at that, where the ultimate particles of matters were conceived as hard, impenetrable, homogeneous little billiard-balls, with no hooks or internal structure. To see how such atoms could combine at all was very hard. Physics, accordingly, moved on from this notion to one which treats atoms and other particles as complex items, describable mainly in terms of forces, and those the same kind of forces which operate outside them. It has abandoned the notion of ultimate, solitary, independent individuals.

Social-contract theory, however, retains it. On this physical – or archaeophysical – model, all significant moral relations between individuals are the symmetrical ones expressed by contract. If, on the other hand, we use a biological or 'organic' model, we can talk also of a variety of asymmetrical relations found within a whole. Leaves relate not only to other leaves, but to fruit, twigs, branches and the whole tree. People appear not only as individuals, but as members of their groups, families, tribes, species, ecosystems and biosphere, and have moral relations, as parts, to these various wholes.

The choice between these two ways of thinking is not, of course, a simple once-for-all affair. Different models are useful for different purposes. We can, however, reasonably point out, first, that the old physical pattern makes all attempts to explain combination extremely difficult. Second, that since human beings actually are living creatures, not crystals or galaxies, it is reasonable to expect that biological ways of thinking will be useful in understanding them.

In its own sphere, the social-contract model has of course been of enormous value. Where we deal with clashes of interest between free and rational agents already in existence, and particularly where we want to disentangle a few of them from some larger group which really does not suit them, it is indispensable. And for certain political purposes during the last three centuries these clashes have been vitally important. An obsession with contractual thinking and a conviction that it is a cure-all are therefore understandable. But the trouble with such obsessions is that they distort the whole shape of thought and language in a way which makes them self-perpetuating, and constantly extends their empire. Terms come to be defined in a way which leaves only certain moral views expressible. This can happen without any clear intention on the part of those propagating them, and even contrary to their occasional declarations, simply from mental inertia.

Thus, John Rawls, having devoted most of his long book to his very subtle and exhaustive contractual view of justice, remarks without any special emphasis near the end that, 'We should recall here the limits of a theory of justice. Not only are many aspects of morality left aside, but no account can be given of right conduct in regard to animals and the rest of nature.'[4]

He concedes that these are serious matters.

> Certainly it is wrong to be cruel to animals and the destruction of a whole species can be a great evil. The capacity for feelings of pleasure and pain and for the forms of life of which animals are capable clearly impose duties of compassion and humanity in their case.

All this is important, he says, and it calls for a wider metaphysical enquiry, but it is not his subject. Earlier in the same passage he touches on the question of permanently irrational human beings, and remarks that it 'may present a difficulty. I cannot examine this problem here, but I assume that the account of equality would not be materially affected.'

Won't it though? It is a strange project to examine a single virtue – justice – without at least sketching in one's view of the vast background of general morality which determines its shape and meaning, including, of course, such awkward and non-contractual virtues as 'compassion and humanity'. It isolates the duties which people owe each other *merely as thinkers* from those deeper and more general ones which they owe each other as beings who feel. It cannot, therefore, fail both to split man's nature and to isolate him from the rest of the creation to which he belongs. Such an account may not be *Hamlet* without the prince, but it is *Hamlet* with half the cast missing, and without the state of Denmark. More exactly, it is like a history of Poland which regards Russia, Germany, Europe and the Roman Church as not part of its subject.

I am not attacking John Rawls's account on its own ground. I am simply pointing out what the history of ethics shows all too clearly – how much our thinking is shaped by what our sages *omit* to mention. The Greek philosophers never really raised the problem of slavery till towards the end of their epoch, and then few of them did so with conviction. This happened even though it lay right in the path of their enquiries into political justice and the value of the individual soul. Christianity did raise that problem, because its social background was different, and because the world was in the Christian era already in turmoil, so that men were not presented with the narcotic of happy stability. But Christianity itself did not, until quite recently, seriously face the problem of the morality of punishment, and particularly of eternal punishment.

This failure to raise central questions was not in either case complete. One can find very intelligent and penetrating criticisms of slavery occurring from time to time in Greek writings – even in Aristotle's defence of that institution.[5] But they are mostly like Rawls's remark here. They conclude 'this should be investigated' some day.' The same thing happens with Christian writings concerning punishment, except that the consideration 'this is a great mystery' acts as an even more powerful paralytic to thought. Not much more powerful, however. Natural inertia, when it coincides with vested interest or the illusion of vested interest, is as strong as gravitation.

Rights and duties

It is important that Rawls does not (like Grice) demand that we toe a line which would make certain important moral views impossible. Like Hume, who similarly excluded animals from justice, he simply leaves them out of his discussion. This move ought in principle to be harmless. But when it is combined with an intense concentration of discussion on contractual justice, and a corresponding neglect of compassion and humanity, it inevitably suggests that the excluded problems are relatively unimportant.

This suggestion is still more strongly conveyed by rulings which exclude the non-human world from rights, duties and morality. Words like *rights* and *duties* are awkward because they do indeed have narrow senses approximating to the legal, but they also have much wider ones in which they cover the whole moral sphere. To say 'They do not have rights' or 'You do not have duties to them' conveys to any ordinary hearer a very simple message, namely, 'They do not matter.' This is an absolution, a removal of blame for ill-treatment of 'them', whoever they may be.

To see how strong this informal, moral usage of 'rights' is, we need only look at the history of that powerful notion, 'the Rights of Man'. These rights were not supposed to be ones conferred by law, since the whole point of appealing to them was to change laws so as to embody them. They were vague, but vast. They did not arise, as rights are often said to do, only within a community, since they were taken to apply in principle everywhere. The immense, and on the whole coherent, use which has been made of this idea by reforming movements shows plainly that the tension between the formal and the informal idea of *right* is part of the word's meaning, a fruitful connection of thought, not just a mistake. It is therefore hard to adopt effectively the compromise which some philosophers now favour, of saying that it is indeed wrong to treat animals in certain ways, but that we have no duties to them or that they have no rights.[6] 'Animal rights' may be hard to formulate, as indeed are the rights of man. But 'no rights' will not do.[7] The word may need to be dropped entirely.

The compromise is still harder with the word *duty*, which is rather more informal, and is more closely wedded to a private rather than political use. Where the realm of right and duty stops, there, to ordinary thinking, begins the realm of the optional. What is not a duty may be a matter of taste, style or feeling, of aesthetic sensibility, of habit and nostalgia, of etiquette and local custom; but it cannot be something which demands our attention whether we like it or not. When claims get into this area, they can scarcely be taken seriously.

This becomes clear when Kant tries to straddle the border. He says that we have no direct duties to animals, because they are not rational, but that we should treat them properly all the same because of 'indirect duties' which are really duties to our own humanity.[8] This means that ill-treating them might lead us to ill-treat humans, and is also a sign of a bad or inhumane disposition. The whole issue thus becomes a contingent one of spiritual style or training, like contemplative exercises, intellectual practice, or indeed refined manners.[9] Some might need practice of this kind to make them kind to people; others might not and indeed might get on better without it. (Working off one's ill-temper on animals might make one treat people *better*.) But the question of cruelty to animals cannot be like this, because it is of the essence of such training exercises that they are internal. Anything that affects some other being is not just practice, it is real action. Anyone who refrained from cruelty *merely* from a wish not to sully his own character, without any direct consideration for the possible victims, would be frivolous and narcissistic.

Trivializing compassion

A similar trivialization follows where theorists admit duties of compassion and humanity to non-contractors, but deny duties of justice. Hume and Rawls, in making this move, do not explicitly subordinate these other duties, or say that they are less binding. But because they make the contract element so central to morality, this effect seems to follow. The priority of justice is expressed in such everyday proverbs as 'Be just before you're generous'. We are therefore rather easily persuaded to think that compassion, humanity and so forth are perhaps emotional luxuries, to be indulged only after all debts are paid.

A moment's thought will show that this is wrong. Someone who receives simultaneously a request to pay a debt and another to comfort somebody bereaved or on their death-bed is not, as a matter of course, under obligation to pay the debt first. He has to look at circumstances on both sides; but in general we should probably expect the other duties to have priority. This is still more true if, on his way to pay the debt, he encounters a stranger in real straits, drowning or lying injured in the road. To give the debt priority, we probably need to think of his creditor as also being in serious trouble – which brings compassion and humanity in on both sides of the case.

What makes it so hard to give justice a different clientele from the other virtues – as Hume and Rawls do – is simply the fact that justice is such a pervading virtue. In general, all serious cases of cruelty, meanness, inhumanity and the like are also cases of injustice. If we are told that a certain set of these cases does not involve injustice, our natural thought is that these cases must be *trivial*. Officially, Hume's and Rawls's restriction is not supposed to mean this. What, however, is it supposed to mean? It is forty years since I first read David Hume's text, and I find his thought as obscure now as I did then. I well remember double-taking then, and going back over the paragraph for a point which I took it I must have missed. Can anyone see it?

> Were there [Hume says] a species of creature intermingled with men, which, though rational, were possessed of such inferior strength, both of body and mind, that they were incapable of all resistance, and could never, upon the highest provocation, make us feel the effects of their resentment; the necessary consequence, I think, is that we should be bound by the laws of humanity to give gentle usage to these creatures, but should not, properly speaking, lie under any restraint of justice with regard to them, nor could they possess any right or property, exclusive of such arbitrary lords. Our intercourse with them could not be called society, which supposes a degree of equality, but absolute command on one side and servile obedience on the other. This is plainly the situation of men with regard to animals.[10]

I still think that the word justice, so defined, has lost its normal meaning. In ordinary life we think that duties of justice become *more* pressing, not less so, when we are dealing with the weak and inarticulate, who cannot argue back. It is the boundaries of prudence which depend on power, not those of justice.

Historically, Hume's position becomes more understandable when one sees its place in the development of social-contract thinking. The doubtful credit for confining justice to the human species seems to belong to Grotius, who finally managed to ditch the Roman notion of *ius naturale*, natural right or law common to all species. I cannot here discuss his remarkably unimpressive arguments for this.[11] The point I want to make here is simply the effect of these restrictive definitions of terms like justice on people's view of the sheer size of the problems raised by what falls outside them.

A vaster scene

Writers who treat morality as primarily contractual tend to discuss non-contractual cases briefly, casually and parenthetically, as though they were rather rare. (Rawls's comments on the problem of mental defectives are entirely typical here.) We have succeeded, they say, in laying most of the carpet; why are you making this fuss about those little wrinkles behind the sofa?

This treatment confirms a view, already suggested by certain aspects of contemporary politics in the United States, that those who fail to clock in as normal rational agents and make their contracts are just occasional exceptions, constituting one more 'minority' group – worrying no doubt to the scrupulous, but not a central concern of any society. Let us, then, glance briefly at their scope, by roughly listing some cases which seem to involve us in non-contractual duties. (The order is purely provisional and the numbers are added just for convenience.)

Human sector
1 The dead
2 Posterity
3 Children
4 The senile
5 The temporarily insane
6 The permanently insane
7 Defectives, ranging down to 'human vegetables'
8 Human embryos

Animal sector
9 Sentient animals
10 Non-sentient animals

Inanimate sector
11 Plants of all kinds
12 Artefacts, including works of art
13 Inanimate but structured objects – crystals, rivers, rocks, etc.

Comprehensive
14 Unchosen human groups of all kinds, including families, villages, cities and the species
15 Unchosen multi-species groups, such as ecosystems, forests and countries
16 The biosphere

Miscellaneous
17 Arts and sciences
18 Oneself
19 God

No doubt I have missed a few, but that will do to go on with.

The point is this. If we look only at a few of these groupings, and without giving them full attention, it is easy to think that we can include one or two as honorary contracting members, by a slight stretch of our conceptual scheme, and find arguments for excluding the others from serious concern entirely. But if we keep our eye on the size of the range, this stops being plausible.

As far as sheer numbers go, this is no minority of the beings with whom we have to deal. We are a small minority of them. As far as importance goes, it is certainly possible to argue that some of these sorts of being should concern us more and others less; we need a priority system. But to build it, *moral* arguments are required. The various kinds of claims have to be understood and compared, not written off in advance. We cannot rule that those who, in our own and other cultures, suppose that there is a direct objection to injuring or destroying some of them, are always just confused, and mean only, in fact, that this item will be needed for rational human consumption.

The blank antithesis which Kant made between rational persons (having value) and mere things (having none) cannot serve us to map out this vast continuum. And the idea that, starting at some given point on this list, we have a general licence for destruction, is itself a moral view which would have to be justified.

Our culture differs from most others in the breadth of destructive licence which it does allow itself, and from the seventeenth century onwards, that licence has been greatly extended. Scruples about rapine have been continually dismissed as irrational, but it is not always clear what the rational principles are supposed to be with which they conflict. Western destructiveness has not in fact developed in response to a new set of disinterested intellectual principles, demonstrating the need for more people and fewer redwoods, but mainly as a by-product of greed and increasing commercial confidence.

Humanistic hostility to superstition has certainly played some part in the process, because respect for the non-human items on our list is often taken to be religious. But it does not have to be. Many scientists who are card-carrying atheists can still see the point of preserving the biosphere. So can the rest of us, religious or otherwise. It is the whole of which we are parts, and its other parts concern us for that reason.

But the language of rights is rather ill-suited for expressing this, because it has been developed mainly for the protection of people who, though oppressed, are in principle articulate. This makes it quite reasonable for theorists to say that rights belong only to those who understand them and can claim them. When confronted with the Human sector of our list, these theorists can either dig themselves in like Grice and exclude the lot, or stretch the scheme like Rawls, by including the hypothetical rational choices which these honorary members *would* make if they were not unfortunately prevented.

Since many of these people seem less rational than many animals, zoophiles like Peter Singer have then a good case for calling this second device arbitrary and specious, and extending rights to the border of sentience.[12] Here, however, the meaning of the term does become thin, and when we reach the inanimate area, usage will scarcely cover it.[13] There may be a point in campaigning to extend usage. But to me it seems wiser on the whole not to waste energy on this verbal point, but instead to insist on the immense variety of kinds of being with which we have to deal. Once we grasp this, we ought not to be surprised that we are involved in many different kinds of claim or duty. The dictum that 'rights and duties are correlative' is quite misleading, because the two words keep different company, and one may be narrowed without affecting the other.

The problem of self-respect

What, then, about duties? I believe that this term can properly be used over the whole range. We have quite simply got many kinds of duties, including those to animals, to plants and to the biosphere. But to speak in this way we must free the term once and for all from its restrictive contractual use, or irrelevant doubts will still haunt us. If we cannot do this, we shall have to exclude the word *duty*, along with *right* (as a noun) from all detailed discussion, using wider words like *wrong, right* (adjectival) and *ought* instead. This gymnastic would be possible but inconvenient.

The issue about duty becomes clear as soon as we look at the controversy from which I started, between Kant's and Mill's views on duties to oneself. What do we think about this? Are there duties of integrity, autonomy, self-knowledge, self-respect? It seems that there are.

Mill was right, of course, to point out that they are not duties *to* someone in the ordinary sense. The divided self is a metaphor. It is as natural and necessary a metaphor here as it is over, say, self-deception or self-control; but it certainly is not literal truth. The form of the requirement is different. Rights, for instance, certainly do not seem to come in here as they often would with duties to other persons; we shall scarcely say, 'I have a right to my own respect.' And the *kind* of things which we can owe ourselves are distinctive. It is not just chance whom they they are owed to. You cannot owe it to somebody else, as you can to yourself, to force him to act freely or with integrity. He owes that to himself; the rest of us can only remove outside difficulties.

As Kant justly said, our business is to promote our own perfection and the happiness of others; the perfection of others is an aim which belongs to them.[14] *Respect* indeed we owe both to ourselves and to others, but Kant may well be right to say that *self-respect* is really a different and deeper requirement, something without which all outward duties would become meaningless. (This may explain the paralysing effect of depression.)

Duties to oneself, in fact, are duties with a different *form*. They are far less close than outward duties to the literal model of debt, especially money debt. Money is a thing which can be owed in principle to anybody; it is the same whoever you owe it to; and if by chance you come to owe it to yourself, the debt vanishes. Not many of our duties are really of this impersonal kind; the attempt to commute other sorts of duty into money is a notorious form of evasion. Utilitarianism, however, wants to make all duties as homogeneous as possible, and that is the point of Mill's position. He views all our self-concerning motives as parts of the desire for happiness. Therefore he places all duty, indeed, all morality, in the outside world, as socially required restriction of that desire – an expression, that is, of other people's desire for happiness.

> We do not call anything wrong, unless we mean that a person ought to be punished in some way or another for doing it; if not by law, by the opinion of his fellow-creatures; if not by opinion, by the reproaches of his own conscience. This seems the real turning-point of the distinction between morality and simple expediency. It is a part of the notion of Duty in every one of its forms, that a person may rightly be compelled to fulfil it. Duty is a thing which may be *exacted* from a person, as one exacts a debt.[15]

But to make the notion of wrongness depend on punishment and public opinion in this way instead of the other way round is wild.

Mill never minded falling flat on his face from time to time in trying out a new notion for the public good. He did it for us here – and we should, I think, take proper advantage of his generosity, and accept the impossibility which he demonstrates. The concepts cannot be connected up this way round. Unless you think of certain facts as wrong, it makes no sense to talk of punishment. 'Punishing' alcoholics with aversion therapy, or experimental rats with electric shocks, is not really punishing at all; it is just deterrence. This 'punishment' will not make their previous actions wrong, nor has it anything to do with morality. The real point of morality returns into Mill's scheme in the Trojan horse of 'the reproaches of his own conscience'. Why do *they* matter? Unless the conscience is talking sense – that is, on Utilitarian principles, unless it is delivering the judgment of society – it should surely be silenced? Mill, himself a man of enormous integrity and deeply concerned about autonomy, would never have agreed to silence it. But unless we do so, we shall have to complicate his scheme.

It may well be true that, in the last resort and at the deepest level, conscience and the desire for happiness converge. We do want to be honest. But in ordinary life and at the everyday level they can diverge amazingly. We do not want to be put out. What we know we ought to do is often most unwelcome to us, which is why we call it *duty*. And whole sections of that duty do not concern other people directly at all.

A good example is the situation in *Brave New World* where a few dissident citizens have grasped the possibility of a fuller and freer life. Nobody else wants this. Happiness is already assured. If there is a duty of change here, it must be first of all that of each to himself. True, they may feel bound also to help others to change, but hardly in a way which those others would *exact*. In fact, we may do better here by dropping the awkward second party altogether and saying that they all have a duty *of* living differently – one which will affect both themselves and others, but which does not require, as a debt does, a named person or people *to* whom it must be paid. Wider models like 'the whole duty of man' may be more relevant.

This one example from my list will, I hope, be enough to explain the point. I cannot go through all of them, nor ought it to be necessary. Duties need not be quasi-contractual relations holding between symmetrical pairs of rational human agents. There are all kinds of other obligations holding between asymmetrical pairs, or involving, as in this case, no outside beings at all.

To speak of duties *to* things in the inanimate and comprehensive sectors of my list is not necessarily to personify them superstitiously, or to indulge in chatter about 'the secret of life of plants'.[16] It expresses merely that there are suitable and unsuitable ways of behaving in given situations. People have duties *as* farmers, parents, consumers, forest-dwellers, colonists, species-members, ship-wrecked mariners, tourists, potential ancestors and actual descendants, etc. As such, it is the business of each not to forget his transitory and dependent position, the rich gifts which he has received, and the tiny part he plays in a vast, irreplaceable and fragile whole.

It is remarkable that we nowadays have to state this obvious truth as if it were new, and invent words like 'ecological' to describe a whole vast class of duties. Most peoples are used to the idea. In stating it, and getting it back into the centre of our moral stage, we meet various difficulties, of which the most insidious is possibly the temptation to feed this issue as fuel to long-standing controversies about religion. Is concern for the non-human aspects of our biosphere necessarily superstitious and therefore to be resisted tooth-and-nail?

I have pointed out that it need not be religious at all. Certified rejectors of all known religions can share it. No doubt there is a wider sense in which any deep and impersonal concern can be called religious – one in which Marxism also is a religion. No doubt too all such deep concerns have their dangers, but certainly the complete absence of them has worse ones. Moreover, anyone wishing above all to avoid the religious dimension should consider that the intense individualism which has focused our attention exclusively on the social-contract model is itself thoroughly mystical. It has glorified the individual human soul as an object having infinite and transcendent value, has hailed it as the only real creator, and has bestowed on it much of the panoply of God.

Nietzsche, who was responsible for much of this new theology,[17] took over from the old Thomistic theology which he plundered the assumption that all the rest of creation mattered only as a frame for man. This is not an impression which any disinterested observer would get from looking round at it, nor do we need it in order to take our destiny sufficiently seriously.

The island's claim

Robinson Crusoe then, I conclude, did have duties concerning his island, and with the caution just given we can reasonably call them duties *to* it.

They were not very exacting, and were mostly negative. They differed, of course, from those which a long-standing inhabitant of a country has. Here the language of *fatherland* and *motherland*, which is so widely employed, indicates rightly a duty of care and responsibility which can go very deep, and which long-settled people commonly do feel strongly. To insist that it is really only a duty to the exploiting human beings is not consistent with the emphasis often given to reverence for the actual trees, mountains, lakes, rivers and the like which are found there. A decision to inhibit all this rich area of human love is a special manoeuvre for which reasons would need to be given, not a dispassionate analysis of existing duties and feelings.

What happens, however, when you are shipwrecked on an entirely strange island? As the history of colonization shows, there is a tendency for people so placed to drop any reverence and become more exploitative. But it is not irresistible. Raiders who settle down can quite soon begin to feel at home, as the Vikings did in East Anglia, and can after a while become as possessive, proud and protective towards their new land as old inhabitants. Crusoe from time to time shows this pride rather touchingly, and it would, I think, certainly have inhibited any moderate temptation such as that which I mentioned to have a good bonfire. What keeps him sane through his stay, however, is in fact his duty to God. If that had been absent, I should rather suppose that sanity would depend on a stronger and more positive attachment to the island itself and its creatures.

It is interesting, however, that Crusoe's story played its part in developing that same unrealistic, icy individualism which has gone so far towards making both sorts of attachment seem corrupt or impossible. Rousseau delighted in Defoe's *Robinson Crusoe*, and praised it as the only book fit to be given to a child, *not* because it showed a man in his true relation to animal and vegetable life, but because it was the bible of individualism.

> The surest way to raise him [the child] above prejudice and to base his judgments on the true relations of things, is to put him in the place of a solitary man, and to judge all things as they would be judged by such a man in relation to their own utility. . . . So long as only bodily needs are recognised, man is self-sufficing . . . the child knows no other happiness but food and freedom![18]

That false atomic notion of human psychology – a prejudice above which nobody ever raised Rousseau – is the flaw in all social-contract thinking. If he were right, every member of the human race would need a separate island, and heaven knows what our ecological problems would be then.

Perhaps, after all, we had better count our blessings.

Notes

Evolutionary dramas

1 Jacques Monod, *Chance and Necessity*, trans. Austryn Wainhouse (London, Fontana, 1974), p. 160.

2 M. T. Ghiselin, *The Economy of Nature and the Evolution of Sex* (Berkeley, Cal., University of California Press, 1974), p. 247.

3 For both these influences see Gillian Beer's excellent discussions in *Darwin's Plots; Evolutionary Narrative in Darwin, George Eliot and Nineteenth Century Fiction* (London, Routledge & Kegan Paul, 1984), especially pp. 30–40 and 83–8.

4 ibid.

5 Quoted by James Moore, *The Post-Darwinian Controversies; A Study of the Protestant Struggle to Come to Terms with Darwin in Great Britain and America 1870–1900* (Cambridge, Cambridge University Press, 1979), p. 167, from Edward Clodd.

6 In his *Philosophie Zoologique* (1809) and *Histoire Naturelle des Animaux sans Vertèbres* (1815–22).

7 This whole process is very well described by Stephen Jay Gould in *The Mismeasure of Man* (New York and London, W. W. Norton, 1981).

8 Chillingly set out in his widely read *Psychological Care of Infant and Child* (New York, W. W. Norton, 1928), and well discussed by B. Ehrenreich and D. English in *For Her Own Good, 150 Years of the Experts' Advice to Women* (London, Pluto Press, 1979).

9 A campaign begun in *Beast and Man; The Roots of Human Nature* (Brighton, Harvester Press, 1979; pbk edn, London, Methuen, 1980) and continued in *Heart and Mind; The Varieties of Moral Experience* (Brighton, Harvester Press, 1981; pbk edn, London, Methuen, 1983).

Do science and religion compete?

1 In *The Post-Darwinian Controversies; A Study of the Protestant Struggle to Come to*

Terms with Darwin in Great Britain and America 1870–1900 (Cambridge Cambridge University Press, 1979).

2 See J. R. Lucas, 'Wilberforce and Huxley; a legendary encounter', *T Historical Journal*, 22,2 (1979), pp. 313–30 for the whole story and p. 318 fc this quotation. Huxley's position and its extremely interesting back ground in his wider thinking are excellently examined in Sheridan Gille and Ann Loades, 'Thomas Henry Huxley; the war between science an religion', *The Journal of Religion*, 61, 3 (July 1981) – an article to which owe a great deal which I would like to acknowledge here.

3 Theodosius Dobzhansky, *The Biology of Ultimate Concern* (Londor Fontana, 1971), p. 96.

4 See his books *The Logic of Scientific Discovery* (rev. edn, Londor Hutchinson, 1968) and *Conjectures and Refutations* (rev. edn, Londor Routledge & Kegan Paul, 1963).

5 In *The Structure of Scientific Revolutions* (Chicago, University of Chicag Press, 1970).

6 I have dealt more fully with the issue of 'facts and values' elsewhere, fc instance in my *Beast and Man; The Roots of Human Nature* (Brightor Harvester Press, 1979), ch. 9, and in 'The absence of a gap between fact and values', *Aristotelian Society Supplementary*, LIV (1980).

3 Demarcation disputes

1 A careful, recent version of this view, which makes quite plain that othe kinds of statement cannot even in principle be reduced to the propositior of physics, let alone ever displaced by them, can be found in Dani Dennett's *Brainstorms* (Brighton, Harvester Press, 1979). The earlie simpler, more reductive form is well seen in U. T. Place's article 'Con sciousness is just brain-processes', *British Journal of Psychology*, (Februar 1956), reprinted in A. Flew (ed.), *Body, Mind and Death* (New York an London, Macmillan, 1964), and J. J. C. Smart's 'Sensations and brai processes', *Philosophical Review* (1959). Even at its most extreme, howeve the theory never licensed the view that it would be possible to sto studying subjects like history by their own peculiar methods. Nor ha anybody else who really attended to the matter ever been able to attac any clear sense to this proposal.

4 The irresistible escalator

1 From William Day, *Genesis on Planet Earth; The Search for Life's Beginnir* (East Lansing, Mich., House of Talos, 1979), pp. 390–2.

2 H. J. Muller, *Out of the Night* (New York, 1935). Quoted by Jonatha Glover in *What Sort of People Should There Be?* (Harmondsworth, Penguir 1984), p. 32.

3 From Francis Darwin and A. C. Seward (eds), *More Letters of Charl Darwin* (London, John Murray, 1903), pp. 338–49.

4 For a good statement of this point, see Stephen Jay Gould, *Ever Sin Darwin* (Harmondsworth, Penguin, 1980), ch. 2.

5 David Duncan (ed.), *The Life and Letters of Herbert Spencer* (London, Williams, & Norgate, 1908), p. 555.
6 Edward Clodd. See A. C. Armstrong, *Transitional Eras in Thought, with Special Reference to the Present Age* (New York, Macmillan, 1904), p. 48.
7 J. D. Bernal, *The World, The Flesh and the Devil* (London, Cape, 1929), pp. 68–73. Quoted by Brian Easlea, *Science and Sexual Oppression* (London, Routledge & Kegan Paul, 1983), pp. 19–21.

5   Choosing a world

1 B. F. Skinner, *Walden Two* (New York, Macmillan, 1948), pp. 96–103 and 248–9.
2 In C. S. Walla (ed.), *Towards Century 21* (New York, Basic Books, 1978).
3 New York, W. W. Norton, 1981.
4 Robert Nozick, *Anarchy, State and Utopia* (Oxford, Blackwell, 1980), p. 313.
5 Jonathan Glover, *What Sort of People Should There Be?* (Harmondsworth, Penguin, 1984).
6 *New Scientist*, 1440 (24 January 1985), p. 58.
7 Theodosius Dobzhansky, *Mankind Evolving* (New Haven, Conn., Yale University Press, 1962) gives an admirable, quite non-technical account of these complexities, and is particularly good in nailing the current misinterpretations and showing how to avoid the crude and hasty conclusions which have again and again been drawn from the earlier theories, in the face of repeated corrections from the geneticists themselves.
8 Glover, op. cit., p. 180.
9 ibid., p. 26.
10 ibid., p. 52.
11 Friedrich Nietzsche, *Thus Spake Zarathustra*, pt 1, 'Of love for one's neighbour', trans. A. Tille and M. Bozman (London, Dent, Everyman edn, 1930).
12 London, Oxford University Press, 1976.

6   The problem of direction

1 Jonathan Glover, *What Sort of People Should There Be?* (Harmondsworth, Penguin, 1984).
2 *Anarchy, State and Utopia* (Oxford, Blackwell, 1980), p. 315n.
3 Glover, op. cit., pp. 32–3.
4 'On the subjectivity and objectivity of knowledge', in John Lewis (ed.), *Beyond Chance and Necessity* (London, Garnstone Press, 1974), pp. 127–8.
5 J. S. Mill, *Essay on Liberty*, ch. 3 (London, Dent, Everyman edn, 1972), pp. 115 and 117.
6 Glover, op. cit., p. 183.
7 B. F. Skinner, *Beyond Freedom and Dignity* (Harmondsworth, Penguin, 1973), pp. 10–12.
8 ibid., pp. 14–16.
9 See Anthony Storr, *Human Aggression* (London, Allen Lane, 1968), pp. 11–14.

7   Scientist and superscientist

1 Francis Crick, *Life Itself, Its Origin and Nature*, (New York, Simon & Schuster, 1981), p. 118.
2 Theodosius Dobzhansky, *The Biology of Ultimate Concern* (London, Fontana, 1971), p. 132.
3 William Day, *Genesis on Planet Earth; The Search for Life's Beginning* (2nd edn, New Haven, Conn., Yale University Press, 1984).
4 See James E. Lovelock, *Gaia; A New Look at the Earth* (London, Oxford University Press, 1974).
5 ibid., pp. 262–4.
6 In *Wickedness; A Philosophical Essay* (London, Routledge & Kegan Paul, 1984), pp. 195–7. For Fromm's discussion, see his *Anatomy of Human Destructiveness* (London, Cape, 1974).

8   Dazzling prospects

1 Edward O. Wilson, *Sociobiology; The New Synthesis* (Cambridge, Mass., Harvard University Press, 1975), pp. 574–5.
2 Julian Huxley, *Religion without Revelation* (London, Benn, 1927), p. 372.
3 See for instance the essay on 'Duties towards animals and spirits' in Kant's *Lectures on Ethics*, trans. Louis Infield (London, Methuen, 1930). I have discussed these difficulties in *Beast and Man* (Brighton, Harvester Press, 1979), pts 4 and 5, and in *Animals and Why They Matter* (Harmondsworth, Penguin, 1983) throughout.
4 William Day, *Genesis on Planet Earth; The Search for Life's Beginning* (2nd edn, New Haven, Conn., Yale University Press, 1984).
5 *Thus Spake Zarathustra*, pt 1, 'Of virtue that giveth', trans. A. Tille and M. Bozman (London, Dent, Everyman edn, 1930), pp. 68–9.
6 *The Antichrist*, sec. 3, trans. R. J. Hollingdale (published with *Twilight of the Idols*) (Harmondsworth, Penguin, 1968), p. 116.
7 *Twilight of the Idols*, sec. 3, 'What the Germans lack', trans. R. J. Hollingdale (Harmondsworth, Penguin, 1968), p. 61.
8 ibid., sec. 29, 'Expeditions of an untimely man', p. 83.
9 Day, op. cit., p. 381.
10 ibid., p. 389.
11 ibid., p. 391.
12 ibid., p. 390.
13 ibid., p. 391.

9   Black holes: Jacques Monod and the isolation of 'science'

1 Steven Weinberg, *The First Three Minutes* (London, André Deutsch, 1977), p. 155.
2 In chapter 1, pp. 1–2.
3 Jacques Monod, *Chance and Necessity*, trans. Austryn Wainhouse (London, Fontana, 1974), p. 50.
4 ibid., pp. 39–40.

5 T. H. Huxley, *Collected Essays* (9 vols) (London, 1894–1908), vol. 5, pp. 73–4.
6 Monod, op. cit., p. 111.
7 In 'Two contrasting world views', in John Lewis (ed.), *Beyond Chance and Necessity* (London, Garnstone Press, 1974), pp. 133–5.
8 A process well explained by C. H. Waddington in 'How much is evolution affected by chance and necessity?' in ibid. See especially p. 94.
9 A point interestingly explained in Freud's *The Future of an Illusion*, trans. Ernest Jones (London, Hogarth Press, 1949), p. 57, where he acknowledges that the religious views which he calls illusions cannot be known to be false, but still rules the name 'illusion' to be suitable because they are known to be wish-fulfilling, therefore childish. But what about the 'illusion' that the universe is intelligible, which makes science possible?

10 Freedom and the Monte Carlo drama

1 See Charles Darwin, *The Descent of Man* (1st edn reprinted, Princeton, NJ, Princeton University Press, 1981), pp. 71–2.
2 Jacques Monod, *Chance and Necessity*, trans. Austryn Wainhouse (London, Fontana, 1974), p. 64.
3 ibid., p. 30.
4 ibid., p. 158.
5 In John Lewis (ed.), *Beyond Chance and Necessity* (London, Garnstone Press, 1974), pp. 126–7.
6 Monod, op. cit., p. 165.
7 ibid., p. 160.
8 Steven Weinberg, *The First Three Minutes* (London, André Deutsch, 1977), p. 154.
9 Monod, op. cit., p. 137; compare also p. 158.

11 Scientific education and human transience

1 Jacques Monod, *Chance and Necessity*, trans. Austryn Wainhouse (London, Fontana, 1974), p. 158.
2 Marcus Aurelius, *Meditations*, X.6 and IV.39, trans. Richard Gray (Bath, 1792).
3 Steven Weinberg, *The First Three Minutes* (London, André Deutsch, 1977), p. 155.
4 Colin Turnbull, *The Human Cycle* (London, Cape, 1984), p. 213.

12 Mixed antitheses

1 Fritdjof Capra, *The Tao of Physics* (London, Wildwood House, 1975) and Gary Zukav, *The Dancing Wu Li Masters* (London, Fontana, 1982).
2 In John Lewis (ed.), *Beyond Chance and Necessity* (London, Garnstone Press, 1974), pp. 128–35.
3 See Peter Reynolds, *On the Evolution of Human Behaviour* (Berkeley, Cal., University of California Press, 1981) pp. 35–6, 68 and 222–4.

4 Stephen Walker, *Animal Thought* (London, Routledge & Kegan Paul, 1983), p. 145.
5 Bertrand Russell, 'Mysticism and logic', reprinted in *Mysticism and Logic* (London, Allen & Unwin, 1917), pp. 9, 10 and 16.
6 London, Gollancz, 1936.

13   Science, scepticism and awe

1 Bertrand Russell, *The Problems of Philosophy* (London, Oxford University Press, 1912–64).
2 David Hume, *Treatise of Human Nature*, ed. P. H. Nidditch (London, Oxford University Press, 1978), p. 270.
3 Bertrand Russell, *Mysticism and Logic* (London, Allen & Unwin, 1917), p. 76.
4 See Wittgenstein's *Philosophical Investigations* (Oxford, Blackwell, 1963).
5 Julian Huxley, *Essays of a Biologist* (London, Chatto & Windus, 1923), pp. 209–10.
6 Russell, 1917, op. cit., p. 29.
7 Theodosius Dobzhansky, *The Biology of Ultimate Concern* (London, Fontana, 1971), pp. 25, 63 and 92.
8 *Life Itself, Its Origin and Nature* (New York, Simon & Schuster, 1981), p. 165.
9 ibid., p. 118.
10 *The Varieties of Religious Experience* (New York, Longman, 1902), p. 56.
11 Edward O. Wilson, *On Human Nature* (Cambridge, Mass., Harvard University Press, 1978), p. 196.
12 ibid., p. 209.
13 Dobzhansky, op. cit., p. 96.
14 Edward O. Wilson, *Sociobiology: The New Synthesis* (Cambridge, Mass., Harvard University Press, 1975), pp. 559–62; 1978, op. cit., p. 192.

14   The service of self and the service of Kali

1 William Sumner, *The Challenge of Facts* (1887), p. 67.
2 Richard Hofstadter, *Social Darwinism in American Thought* (New York, Braziller, 1959), p. 47.
3 H. Trevor-Roper (ed.), *Hitler's Table-Talk* (London, Weidenfeld & Nicolson, 1963).
4 Charles Darwin, *The Descent of Man* (reprinted, Princeton, NJ, Princeton University Press, 1981).
5 A view which first appeared in his *Natural Selection and Tropical Nature; Essays on Descriptive and Theoretical Biology* (London, Macmillan, 1891) and increasingly pervaded his later work. Wallace had been converted from his earlier Darwinian position by spiritualism. See James R. Moore, *The Post-Darwinian Controversies; A Study of the Protestant Struggle to Come to Terms with Darwin in Great Britain and America 1870–1900* (Cambridge, Cambridge University Press, 1979) pp. 184–7.
6 See its third chapter, especially the opening few pages.

7 Edward O. Wilson, *Sociobiology; The New Synthesis* (Cambridge, Mass., Harvard University Press, 1975), p. 3.

15 Who or what is selfish?

1 Richard Dawkins, *The Selfish Gene* (London, Oxford University Press, 1976), pp. 2–3.
2 Edward O. Wilson, *Sociobiology; The New Synthesis* (Cambridge, Mass., Harvard University Press, 1975), p. 3.
3 Dawkins, op. cit., p. 36.
4 ibid., p. 64.
5 Edward O. Wilson, *On Human Nature* (Cambridge, Mass., Harvard University Press, 1978), pp. 155–6.
6 Wilson, 1975, op. cit., p. 157.
7 M. T. Ghiselin, *The Economy of Nature and the Evolution of Sex* (Berkeley, Cal., University of California Press, 1974), p. 247.
8 David Barash (London, Souvenir Press, 1980).
9 ibid., p. 3.
10 David Barash, *Sociology and Behaviour* (New York, Elsevier-North Holland Publishing, 1977).
11 Wilson, 1975, op. cit., pp. 3–4.
12 ibid., p. 3.
13 Barash, 1977, op. cit., p. 70.
14 Wilson, 1978, op. cit., p. 167.
15 Jacques Monod, *Chance and Necessity*, trans. Austryn Wainhouse (London, Fontana, 1974), p. 45.
16 Nicholas Tinbergen, *The Study of Instinct* (London, Oxford University Press, 1951; new introduction 1969), pp. vi–x.

16 Dreaming and waking

1 See Paul R. Ehrlich, Carl Sagan, Donald Kennedy and Walter Orr Roberts, *The Cold and the Dark; The World After Nuclear War* (London, Sidgwick & Jackson, 1984), well reviewed in *New Scientist* (4 October 1984).

17 The limits of individualism

1 See his admirable book *Man's Responsibility for Nature* (London, Duckworth, 1974) pp. 54–6 and 110–26.
2 C. S. Lewis, *The Screwtape Letters* (London, Geoffrey Bles, 1942), p. 129.

18 The vulnerable world and its claims on us

1 J. S. Mill, *Essay on Liberty*, ch. 4 (London, Dent, Everyman edn, 1972), p. 135.

2 Essay on 'Duties to oneself' in *Lectures on Ethics*, trans. Louis Infield (London, Methuen, 1930), p. 118.

3 *Grounds of Moral Judgment* (Cambridge, Cambridge University Press, 1967), pp. 146–7.

4 John Rawls, *A Theory of Justice* (London, Oxford University Press, 1972), p. 512.

5 Aristotle, *Politics*, I, 3–8; compare *Nicomachean Ethics* VII, 11.

6 For instance John Passmore, *Man's Responsibility for Nature* (London, Duckworth, 1974), pp. 116–17 and H. J. McCloskey, 'Rights', *Philosophical Quarterly*, 15 (1965).

7 Nor will it help for philosophers to say 'it is not the case that they have rights'. Such pompous locutions have either no meaning at all, or the obvious one.

8 In 'Duties towards animals and spirits' in Kant, op. cit.

9 A point well discussed by Stephen Clark in *The Moral Status of Animals* (London, Oxford University Press, 1977), pp. 12–13.

10 *Enquiry Concerning the Principles of Morals* (1777), s. 152.

11 For details see John Rodman, 'Animal justice; the counter-revolution in natural rights and law', *Inquiry*, 22, 1–2 (summer 1979).

12 A case first made by Jeremy Bentham, *An Introduction to the Principles of Morals and Legislation*, ch. 17, and ably worked out by Peter Singer in *Animal Liberation* (London, Cape, 1976), chs 1, 5 and 6.

13 It is worth noticing that long before this, when dealing merely with the rights of man, the term often seems obscure, because to list and specify those rights is so much harder than to shout for them. The phrase is probably more useful as a slogan, indicating a general direction, than as a detailed conceptual tool.

14 Kant, 'Preface to the metaphysical elements of ethics', *Introduction to Ethics*, chs 4 and 5.

15 J. S. Mill, *Utilitarianism*, ch. 5 (London, Dent, Everyman edn, 1972), p. 45.

16 The book so titled, by Peter Tompkins and Christopher Bird (Harmondsworth, Penguin, 1975) claimed to show, by various experiments involving electrical apparatus, that plants can feel. Attempts to duplicate these experiments have, however, failed entirely to produce any similar results. See A. W. Galson and C. L. Slayman, 'The not so secret life of plants', *American Scientist*, 67, p. 337. It seems possible that the original results were due to a fault in the electrical apparatus.

The attempt shows, I think, one of the confusions which continually arise from insisting that all duties must be of the same form. We do not need to prove that plants are animals in order to have reason to spare them. The point is well discussed by Marian Dawkins in her book *Animal Suffering* (London, Chapman & Hall, 1981), pp. 117–19.

17 See particularly *Thus Spake Zarathustra*, pt 3, 'Of old and new tables', trans. A. Tille and M. Bozman (London, Dent, Everyman edn, 1930) and *The Joyful Wisdom* (otherwise called *The Gay Science*) § 125, 'The madman's speech'. I have discussed this rather odd appointment of man to succeed God in an essay called 'Creation and originality' in my *Heart*

and Mind; The Varieties of Moral Experience (Brighton, Harvester Press, 1981).

18 Jean-Jacques Rousseau, *Emile*, trans. Barbara Foxley (London, Dent, Everyman edn, 1966), pp. 147–8.

Index